T0142582

BUT GOD

A Bible Study on Joshua

Dawn Keister

WESTBOW
PRESS®
A DIVISION OF THOMAS NELSON
& ZONDERVAN

All scripture quotations are taken from the Holy Bible, New International Version®, NIV®. Copyright ©
1973, 1978, 1984, 2011 by Biblica, Inc.™ Used by permission of Zondervan. All rights reserved worldwide.
WestBow Press books may be ordered through booksellers or by contacting:

WestBow Press
A Division of Thomas Nelson & Zondervan
1663 Liberty Drive
Bloomington, IN 47403
www.westbowpress.com
1 (866) 928-1240

ISBN: 978-1-5127-9960-6 (sc)
ISBN: 978-1-5127-9959-0 (e)

Library of Congress Control Number: 2017912464

Print information available on the last page.

WestBow Press rev. date: 09/12/2017

Dedication

To Jesus, the irrevocable love of my life. You have been faithful even when I am not. In the words of the apostle Paul, "I consider my life worth nothing to me. If only I may finish the race and complete the task You have given me—the task of testifying to the gospel of God's grace" (Acts 20:24). May I forever be in pursuit of You and be willing to surrender it all for Your fame.

Acknowledgments

To my four beautiful, beloved children—you provide endless delight and laughter to my every day. May you passionately pursue God's plan in your lives, and may you love Him with all your hearts, souls, minds, and strength. You have exemplified love and encouragement through this entire process. I love you all with all of my heart.

To Stef—you believed in my dream and God's call on my life, and you enabled it to come to fruition.

To my "Fierce in the Faith" Friday night small group—thanks for being the trial run, the guinea pigs of this study. Your prayers and encouragement are priceless.

PREFACE

I have always dreamed of being a writer. From the time I was a little girl, I felt the itch to pick up a pen and open to a blank sheet of paper and write, and I did! To me, there was nothing in the world like a fresh sheet of paper and the smell of ink on the pages. I would write a neighborhood newspaper (much to the chagrin of my neighbors, who regularly were my interviewees). As I grew older, my writing turned more inwardly focused, and I chose to journal about everything. I always said that one day I would write a book. I am a firm believer that God placed in my heart the passion for writing from a young age—though at the time, I could not envision in what capacity it would be used. In my mid-twenties, I felt God pushing me in the direction of women's ministry. I resisted the call and had to endure some painful situations as a result. He offered me, as He offers every one of you, the gift of forgiveness and the opportunity to right my relationship with Christ Jesus. Fast forward to the summer of 2016, and God was not letting me escape what He had written on my heart. How could I not share with other women my love for Jesus? I love Bible study. I love digging into God's Word and letting it saturate to the core of my being. I love learning of His words and His instruction for my life. Yet last summer, God told me it was time to set aside the other studies and focus on hearing Him and what He had to say to me and through me. I knew I would not resist His call this time.

I have always felt a connection with Peter and his story. I was so excited and just knew without a doubt that this would be the subject of the Bible study. Yet as I prayed and sought God's direction, He seemed to be saying to me, "Joshua." At first, I was convinced I had not heard correctly and subsequently had that entertaining dialogue with God. He made it clearly known that, yes indeed, the subject was to be on the story of Joshua and the nation of Israel's journey into the Promised Land. Prior to preparing for this study, I really had not studied Joshua's role in the nation of Israel's claim to their inheritance. I just kept hearing the childhood tune of "Joshua fought the battle of Jericho, Jericho, Jericho." What I would have missed out on had I not chosen the path of obedience. As you begin this Bible-study journey, I pray God will bless your heart beyond measure, and you will learn everyday life lessons. Thank you, and I will be praying for you!

Dawn

WEEK 1

Day 1

Verse of the day: "Only do not rebel against the LORD. And do not be afraid of the people of the land, because we will swallow them up. Their protection is gone, but the LORD is with us. Do not be afraid of them" (Numbers 14:9).

In Numbers 13 and 14, Joshua and Caleb were sent as spies to survey the land of Canaan. Based upon their account, they acknowledged the Lord's protection over Israel and His ability to give them the victory. How did the nation of Israel respond to their report? Their response was a desire to stone them (just *what*?) The nation of Israel then wandered for forty years in the wilderness because they were not willing to trust God to provide protection and victory. Yet Joshua (and Caleb) had faith in their God and that He would go with them and they would not be defeated! What made Joshua different? While others found excuses or the threat of danger stronger than God's protection, why did Joshua believe in God's protection?

Read Joshua 1:6–9.

The Lord promises to never leave Joshua—He tells him to meditate on the Law, day and night. He tells Joshua to be strong and courageous. He tells Joshua to not be frightened. He promises to be with Joshua wherever he goes.

Joshua was Moses's assistant, and he witnessed firsthand all that God did for Moses and God's faithfulness to the children of Israel. He believed God to be true to His promises. He knew God would be faithful. The Israelites wandered in the wilderness for forty years because they didn't believe God. Over and over, they seemed to quickly forget all that God had done for them. Joshua was different. He believed God's promises.

Isn't that a little bit like us? We pray for God to come through on something for us, and then He does. We thank Him. After some time passes, things come up, life returns to normal, and we quickly forget all that God has done for us. We turn against God with an attitude of negativity and complaining, saying, "Really, God? Again?" And we forget that God may be giving us the opportunity to trust in Him, to change our attitudes and reactions to whatever it is we are facing. Imagine God's delight if we were to say to Him, "Lord, I don't know why or how, but I know who, and that is You. You want good things for me. So I am choosing to trust You, even in this." What if this was our first response? How different our challenges or hardships might seem! God promised Joshua that He would not leave him and that he should have courage. We have the same promise. God will never leave us or forsake us (Hebrews 13:5).

What does God want you to believe about today?

Is there a specific area of your life in which God wants you to be strong and have courage because He is faithful?

As we explore the book of Joshua together, we will discover what made Joshua different, how God demonstrated His faithfulness to the nation of Israel, and how He demonstrates it to us. The journey is just beginning, and it is going to be quite an adventure. I'm so glad you chose to join me for the journey!

Day 2

Verse of the day: "But the woman had taken the two men and hidden them. She said, 'Yes, the men came to me, but I did not know where they had come from'" (Joshua 2:4).

Read Joshua 2.

I love the way our God works and whom He chooses to use, don't you? This account in scripture is so rich and full of hope. God amazes me with His willingness to use the people He chooses. He looks for a heart that is ripe and ready. Rahab was a prostitute—her claim to fame, her descriptor, throughout the Bible—yet her heart was ready and softened to receive God and have faith in Him. She stepped out in faith, hid the spies, and continued to believe them and their pact with her. She reiterated what God had done for the Israelites, and that fueled her faith. She had heard of God's power and miraculous acts among the nation of Israel. She was faced with a choice—to believe in this God of Israel and offer protection to the spies or to turn them in to save herself. We know what she chose, and that decision is what saved her life as well as her soul! Sister, God will use anyone whose faith is present and who is willing to believe Him, day by day, and do His work. The story of Rahab stirs a tender place in my heart. She did what she believed was right. She believed God, even though she was a prostitute. She could have let who she was and the decisions of her life prevent her from stepping out in faith and believing God. *But God*—His power was already at work in her life. He had plans to use her for His will to be accomplished. Isn't that just like God? How I love Him and how He chooses to work!

How often do we let our pasts define our futures?

What is in your past (or present) that makes you take a step back and say, "Because of this, God can't (or won't) use me"?

Oftentimes we choose to believe the lies of the enemy that we aren't good enough, or our past is too shameful for God to use us. Perhaps we hid behind those lies because of our fear of stepping out in faith to believe that God can use us. We allow Satan's lies to become our excuses to not do God's work or what He has called us to do. Look at the life of Jesus—He came to save the lost, to redeem lives. Not one of us is perfect. If we were, then we would not need Jesus and His sacrifice on the cross. Rahab could have said, "I am merely a prostitute—how could God even know who I am or care to save me?" But she didn't. She chose to believe the spies she hid and, ultimately, to believe God. At the time she made this choice, she couldn't have known how that choice impacted her life for the future. Yet she did it anyway. She could not have imagined that thousands of years later, her name would be remembered, and she would be a source in a Bible study.

How different would our lives look if we chose to believe God?

Where is God prompting your heart to act, to move, and to believe?

Sometimes we fear failure, and that prevents us from doing what we know in our hearts God wants us to do. Sometimes we fear God may not show up, and He will let us down. Isn't that really where the crux of our fears lies? We are afraid God won't show up—yet therein is the beauty of faith. Our God is faithful—without fail. Read the beauty in the verses of Lamentations 3:22–26. Our God is a God who shows up, follows through on His promises, and acts. Praise Him!

Day 3

Verse of the day: "Before the spies lay down for the night, she went up on the roof and said to them, 'I know that the LORD has given this land to you and that a great fear has fallen on us, so that all who live in this country are melting in fear because of you'" (Joshua 2:8–9).

Rahab's life is full of lessons for us through her actions and beliefs. Rahab was a woman in a culture that did not respect women. She was a prostitute. The spies showed up at her doorstep, most likely because they could blend in and gather information from others present. When I picture this scene, I imagine it's set in the Old West. The spies enter a tavern, where they drink together at tables, and prostitutes are milling about. The spies get a feel for the town and the climate by eating a meal and listening to the stories of the locals. This is how I visualize the scene—but of course it wasn't like that.

Rahab could have turned them away or turned them in. She did *not* have to make the choice to hide them. In fact, they made no preemptive promises to her. They didn't say, if you hide us, we will save you when we return. It was only after she sent away those pursuing the spies that they made an oath. My question that underscores this entire study is this: what made her choose differently? And Joshua—what made him act and believe differently than all the other Israelites? What made Rahab, a non-Jew, believe the God of the Israelites rather than protect her own people? Have you ever considered that? What renown our God has!

It is what we choose to do with what we know about God. Rahab had knowledge of God; she had heard the stories (see Joshua 2). Her countrymen responded in fear. Her response was faith. She chose to believe that God could change her. Joshua saw what God had done and of what He was capable when Joshua was Moses's assistant. What did Joshua choose to do with God? Joshua chose to believe that the God who performed mighty miracles would show up in His really big God way, perform miracles, and *show up for him*! Fear and faith are two options we always face when choosing to do what we know God has placed on hearts to do.

Which is your most common response—fear or faith?

Why do you think that is your response?

The Israelites had the same knowledge of God—they witnessed what God had done for them yet they did nothing with it. They quickly forgot what God had done for them, and they stopped believing Him and started complaining.

Read James 2:14–17.

We are told that faith without works is dead. Faith requires action. I can say I believe God and say He can do this or that. It is my actions, however, that reveal my true measure of faith. Am I going to truly surrender and let go of the reins, or am I going to help out God by doing it the way I think it should be done? It is one thing to say I believe God and another to live like I believe God. The warning of the Israelites is how quickly we can lose faith and forget all that God has done for us. When things grow difficult again, we have the choice either to complain and pitch a terrible tantrum or to trust in God's faithfulness. What happens when we don't step out in action when we feel God prompting our hearts to obedience? We are the ones who miss out, just like Israel. They never did get to enter the Promised Land, nor did Moses, because of their unbelief.

Sometimes we get so caught up in our lives and what we want God to do that we don't take the time to ask God what He wants for us or to listen for His response. God's Promised Land and His abundant life for us is so much better than anything we could create or envision for ourselves, but often we lose sight of that because our focus has narrowed so much that we see only what we think our version of the Promised Land should be.

Do you believe God's Promised Land cannot even begin to register in our wildest imaginations?

The time will come for each one of us to throw down our scarlet cords, let go of our ideas of safety, step out in faith, and believe God's promises for our lives, just like Rahab. Why the scarlet cord? A bright scarlet cord stood out among the rubble. Make your life stand out among the rubble of the world around you—in your home, your workplace, your church, your community.

How far-reaching were the effects of Rahab's faith? Tomorrow we will discover them.

Day 4

Verse of the day: "She lives among the Israelites to this day" (Joshua 6:25).

Rahab was not forgotten after the defeat of Jericho. Her faith landed her forever in the history of Israel on the pages of scripture.

Read Joshua 6:17–25.

As you read this account of Rahab and her role in the defeat of Jericho, doesn't the question linger in the back of your mind, "Why Rahab? Why was she so well regarded and remembered for merely hiding the spies? She even lied about it!" But isn't that just like God? He loves to use the most unexpected means to accomplish His purposes. Also, He chooses to use those who are *willing* and whose hearts are *soft*. Sure, Rahab lied. But that's not something to get all tripped up on. Deceit was not an uncommon war tactic. Perhaps deceit isn't the word to describe it—cunning, maybe. However, Rahab hid the spies, sent them on their merry way, hung the scarlet cord from her window, and awaited their return to save her and her family.

Read Matthew 1. What is found here?

Read Matthew 1:5. Who is listed in this genealogy?

Rahab. There's her name. Once the dust settled from the walls of Jericho tumbling down, Rahab married an Israelite and became the mother of Boaz, who married Ruth. Rahab was the great-grandmother of King David, who, of course, is the line from which Jesus Christ was born. Yes, you read that right. Rahab the prostitute was the ancestor of King David and our Savior, Jesus.

The key factor is not that Rahab just hid the spies—which was huge—but it is the heart and faith issue behind the action.

Hebrews 11 is well known as the Hall of Faith in scripture. Read Hebrews 11:31. Rahab was recognized for her *faith* when she hid the spies. That's right—hiding the spies was an act of faith. Perhaps we need to begin thinking outside the box where faith is concerned. It doesn't always come in neat packaging, tied up with a bow. Sometimes, acting in faith is not even perceivable to the unobserving eye. It is the little actions that only we know God is prompting us to take. When we are faithful in the little things, God begins to give us the bigger things. Sometimes, faith appears a little risky and outright preposterous to others. Hiding the spies was an act of faith. Rahab was acknowledged in Hebrews 11 for her faith in hiding the spies ... right smack dab in the middle of the acts of faith of the patriarchs. How awesome is our God. If that doesn't recharge your faith batteries, then have them checked!

Hebrews is not the only place in the New Testament that speaks of our Rahab. Turn to James 2:25. Read it. Now read it again.

Rahab was considered _____ for what she did when she gave the spies lodging. *Righteous*. She took a leap of faith when the people all around her lived in fear of the Israelites. She. Hid. The. Spies. *Faith*. Rahab continues to be remembered today as Rahab the prostitute. Why is she not remembered as Rahab the Righteous? By the time she is discussed in the New Testament, she was considered righteous for her faith.

God doesn't want our list of excuses when He calls us to act. God wants our obedience. Rahab was rewarded for her obedience. In our culture, we tend to balk a little at the word obedience. We want to be our very own bosses. We don't want to obey anyone or submit to the will of others. How contrary to what God requires of us as believers. In scripture, we are called to humbly submit to God. We are called to be obedient to God.

The challenge is whether or not we believe God enough to be obedient, even when it is uncomfortable or scary. Rahab was not even a Jew. She didn't have the intimate knowledge of God the children of Israel had. Yet she obeyed God and acted in faith when she hid the spies. What was the reward of her faith? She was the great-grandmother of King David. She is listed in the genealogy of the Savior of the world and of all humanity.

God uses willing, obedient hearts. He doesn't pick only the ones whose pasts are pristine and without stain. No, our God doesn't work that way. God is scandalous. He looks for hearts that are fully surrendered to Him. He wants our faith and our obedience. He redeems our pasts, regardless of what is in them.

It is time to let go of our excuses, our shame, our guilt ... whatever the "it" is that is preventing us from acting out our faith and taking the step into God's Promised Land for our lives. It is time to offer ourselves up to God as living sacrifices to use for His glory and His fame.

What is your barrier today?

Name it. What is your go-to excuse?

Throw it down before God. Surrender it. He can be trusted with your surrendered heart.

Day 5

Verse of the day: "Remember not the sins of my youth or my transgressions; according to your steadfast love remember me, for the sake of your goodness, O LORD!" (Psalm 25:7).

As I sit here and consider all that has been read and studied this week, I am humbled to the point of tears and overwhelmed by the goodness of God, the mercy of God, the forgiveness of God, and the *grace* of God. Grace is such a beautiful word. It fills my soul with gratitude.

I wonder if Rahab was overwhelmed by the grace of God as she watched His grace unfold in her life through her children, grandchildren, and great-grandchildren. Did she live long enough to see David become king? How interesting to read the words from the psalm above in light of knowing that Rahab's ancestor penned those words! Remember not the sins of my youth. Praise You, Jesus, that You don't remember them. But praise You, Jesus, that I do, so that I don't ever wander back down that path again.

For so many years I hid behind the excuse that God could never use me because my past was far too dark and full of shameful acts to ever be used for His glory. God has just been waiting for me to realize that it was exactly my past that He wanted to use because it brought me here today, to this place of surrender and obedience. I love Him so much because He loved me so much and forgave me so much. Not only did I hide behind excuses, but I also hid behind my own fear. My fear of failure. My fear of finally stepping out and then realizing that perhaps I had heard God wrong. My fear that maybe God would not show up and meet me in that place where faith meets action. But then God said to my heart, "It. Is. Time." How do I deny that voice, that command? I don't. So I stepped out in faith. Every day I resist the urge to pick up a Bible study another has written, one that I know is full of great things that could fuel my faith. Instead, I pick up my reading in Joshua, plant myself before a blank page, and say, "Okay, God. Here I am. No matter how elementary or disconnected the words and thoughts are, I am waiting to hear what You have to say to me through Joshua's story."

Now it's your turn. Where are you today? What are the barriers in your life that are preventing you from not only stepping out in faith but also believing what God has planned for you? Sometimes we can't step out in faith because we don't believe what God is saying to us, or we simply don't want to believe what God is telling us.

Are you able to believe God?

If not, list what you struggle to believe about God or what He is saying.

If you do believe God, what is preventing you from stepping out in faith today?

Pour your heart out to God in a time of reflection. Offer up to Him your fears, your excuses, and your unbelief. Believe God and expect great things from Him for your life. Only expect the unexpected.

Father, we thank You today that You are the God of wonders. We thank you that you are the God who is greater than all of our fears. You are the God who forgives sins. You are the God who redeems our lives from the pit. You are the God who can and will do more than we ask, expect, or imagine. Lord, today, we are offering up our hearts to you, softened and in full surrender. Only You know where this journey leads. We entrust ourselves to You today.

WEEK 2

Day 1

Verse of the day: "Consecrate yourselves for tomorrow the Lord will do wonders among you" (Joshua 3:5).

Read Joshua 3–4.

Reading the Old Testament reignites an awe for the miracles that God works. It is easy to recount the miracles of Christ in the New Testament and not ever link them to the same God who performed miracles in the Old Testament. The face of the miracles just looks different between the two, yet the same. God is the same yesterday (and that means *all* of yesterdays past), today, and forever. That same God still works miracles today—again. They just look different to us and in how we define miracles. Yes, our God is more than able to heal instantaneously yet He doesn't always choose to do so. It's not as much about the miracle as it is the purpose behind the miracle— or lack thereof. When you take the time to consider the miracles in the Bible and examine what the ultimate purpose was, it makes sense that we don't see God act and move exactly as He did in biblical times. In this passage in Joshua, for example, the parting of the Jordan River was to reaffirm and to strengthen their faith in God, who had promised them victory to finally claim their Promised Land. Remember this had not yet happened when they crossed the Jordan.

Read Joshua 4:24.

What does it say was the purpose of the stones at Gilgal?

In the New Testament, Jesus performed countless miracles. He was manifesting Himself as the chosen One, the anointed One, the King, the Redeemer, and the Savior who finally came to seek and to save all who were lost. Ultimately, in each circumstance, the purpose was to bring glory to God. How better to glorify God than to set up stones of remembrance in order to not forget all He has done for us!

Consider your own life. Can you remember times in your life when you knew God supernaturally acted in a way that could only be Him?

Write here about what God did.

As you reflect on this experience, what can you identify as the purpose of God's movement in your life through this?

Take a moment to thank Him for His constant and continuous movement in your life.

Prior to the Israelites crossing the Jordan River, Joshua told the people of Israel to consecrate themselves because God was going to do great things for them "tomorrow." In the original Hebrew language, the word consecrate is *Qadas*, which means "to be clean ... to sanctify, purify ... essentially denotes being pure or devoted to God. Signifies an act or a state in which people or things are set aside and reserved exclusively for God."[1] Old Testament law required the children of Israel to purify themselves for various offerings. As believers, we too are required to consecrate ourselves to God. What does that look like for me and for you? Live in such a way that your life is set apart, and you act, think, speak, and live in such a way that God is glorified and His name is honored. Let there be no question to whom You belong and that you live differently than the world around you. Our culture embraces individuality and being different, as long as it doesn't threaten the way other people live or call it wrong. "To each his own" seems to be the motto of our days. However, God's desire is that believers consecrate themselves in the middle of a culture that no longer views God as King. Set apart yourself, exclusively reserved for God.

Is there an area of your life that you are withholding from God's sanctifying work?

If so, what is it?

Regardless of whether your answer above is yes or no, what is one thing you can do today to begin making a conscious effort to consecrate yourself to God?

God's purpose and ultimate goal is for us to glorify Him with our lives. We can only learn how to glorify Him through our lives by living in close, intimate relationship with Him. He wants us to delight ourselves in Him, and He receives glory from it. Praise be to Jesus!

Day 2

Verse of the day: "So that all the peoples of the earth may know that the hand of the Lord is mighty, that you may fear the Lord your God forever" (Joshua 4:24).

Even as I wrote the words for a fresh day, thoughts lingered about consecrating ourselves to God. Consecration is such an intimate, beautiful, and precious gift that we give not only to our Father but also to ourselves. As believers, we can grow accustomed to certain words or phrases of the faith, and the impact of those words becomes lost on us. As a result, what we completely miss out on is saddening, and we don't even realize it. Consecration is sacred. It is an act of worship. It is a conscious decision to set ourselves apart. We should daily set ourselves apart, cultivate a lifestyle of listening to God's voice, and then act on it. I have meditated on that and let the responsibility I have to consecrate myself really permeate my heart and soul. If you are continually in communication with God, asking Him to show you where you can set yourself apart, it will be worth it.

Whether you're a new believer or have been walking with Christ for years, you have most likely heard the phrase "the fear of the Lord." The Hebrew word used in the passage in Joshua is *Yare,* and it means "to be afraid, to fear, to revere, to terrify, make afraid."[2] This type of fear can also be described as a very positive feeling of awe or reverence for God. Again, "the fear of the Lord" is one of those phrases of the faith that has the potential to lose its meaning in our individual lives. Our culture and even our Christian communities and circles emphasize what a loving and forgiving God we have. And boy, is He ever a loving, compassionate, gracious, and forgiving God. He is also powerful and *holy.* He is the God of the universe who demands and commands our utmost respect. God is by no means a weak God or a passive Father. Jesus can be portrayed and perceived as weak if the loving and compassionate components of His character are not properly balanced with the characteristics of His holiness.

Read Isaiah 6:1–7.

Who did Isaiah see in this passage?

What were the seraphs calling to one another?

How did Isaiah respond in this vision?

When Isaiah was confronted with the holiness of Almighty God, his awareness of his own sinfulness was brought to the surface, and he realized just how unworthy he was. His response was, "Woe to me! I am ruined! For I am a man of unclean lips" (Isaiah 6:5). Who we are without the blood of Christ covering us is made glaringly evident when we encounter the presence of God. God wants us to approach Him with reverence yet with intimacy, both at the same time. Every time we enter the presence of God, we are standing on holy ground. God is a compassionate and loving God, but He is also a holy God. There is nothing within us, nothing of our own merit that allows us access to God. We can only ever approach God and withstand His holiness due to the blood of Jesus Christ that presents us to Christ as pure, spotless, and unblemished.

Nothing we ever could possibly do would be enough to allow us access and entry to the presence of our holy Father. This alone should fill us with so much awe that we approach God with humility and gratitude. He has replaced our unworthiness with acceptance. Not only can we enter God's presence and approach His throne, but we also can have an intimate personal relationship with Him. How awesome is that? How mind-blowing is that? When I consider my own life and my own unworthiness before Him, my brain and my heart can hardly fathom that God chose me, God wants me, God desires a relationship with me, and God uses me to do *His* work. He wants that for you too.

Now, take a moment (or several) and respond to God with how this makes you feel. Even if you're confused about how this makes you feel, tell Him. He wants to hear. He wants to draw you closer to Him. James 4:8 says, "Come near to God, and He will come near to you."

Read 2 Samuel 6:1–9.

What did David decide to do in this passage?

How was the ark transported?

What was Uzzah's fatal mistake?

Upon a first read through of this passage, it is a little shocking to discover the consequences of Uzzah's actions. Let's backpedal for a minute. First of all, the ark of God was not transported according to specific instructions that were set forth in the Law that was given to Moses. Second, in Old Testament times, the ark of God was truly where the presence of God would camp among the children of Israel. What is today's lesson discussing? It's living our lives with a fear and reverence for God's holiness. Uzzah disregarded the proper means of transportation. And in an effort to prevent the ark from falling over, he touched it. God's anger was kindled against Uzzah for such a lack of reverence for the holiness of God. Approaching God should never be taken lightly. God created us for intimate relationships with Him, but we never should lose sight of His holiness and who He is. Over and over again in scripture, we are told of the significance and impact of fearing the Lord. We are not to be afraid of God; that is not at all what He wants for us. No, God wants us to know Him and to revere His holiness. Every single time we approach the throne of God, we should do so with an awe of who He is and a humility that is indicative of the state of our souls without Him in our lives.

Are you able to embrace an intimate relationship with God while never losing sight of who He is or His holiness? Do you lean more toward seeing God as a compassionate, loving Father, and you don't really value and revere His holiness as you ought? God is a perfect God. He is the perfect balance of being both holy and compassionate and forgiving. I'm so thankful for that today. Aren't you? Where would you be without a holy God who is both compassionate and full of grace?

As we close today, reflect on how you personally view God and approach Him.

Praise You, Jesus. Praise You! Let us be like the Israelites under Joshua's leadership that all peoples will know the mighty hand of the Lord and live in holy fear of Him and His complete *greatness*! Amen and amen.

Day 3

Verse of the day: "That day the LORD exalted Joshua in the sight of all Israel; and they revered him all the days of his life, just as they had revered Moses" (Joshua 4:14).

Joshua took over the reins of his leadership with confidence and with a heart set ablaze for doing the work of the Lord. We saw last week how Joshua sent the spies into Jericho to scout out the land. Joshua knew that God had already promised them victory and entry into the Promised Land after their forty years of wandering, but prior to that, Joshua set a precedent for how things needed to move forward. He knew some things needed to be changed and fixed before moving on. We are going to look at what he did and how we can follow his example.

1. Prior to God's acting in mighty ways, Joshua instructed the people to consecrate themselves. We looked at Joshua 3:5 on day one of this week, and we talked about the significance of consecrating ourselves to God and how important it is for us, as believers, to do that so that God can act in mighty ways in our lives.

Read 1 Peter 1:13–15.

Preparing ourselves for battle was not merely an Old Testament concept. The children of Israel were literally consecrating themselves prior to entering the physical and literal battlefield. Don't we too face a battlefield daily? Every single day, we rise up from our beds, and we have an enemy who is determined to derail us from the life God has called us to live. We don't win wars by not preparing for the battle. We will not defeat the enemy of our souls without first doing what Peter calls us to do. He says to "prepare your minds for action." Determine first in your head what it is you're going to do. Examine your heart, your thoughts, and your life to know where your greatest area of weakness is and where you are most vulnerable to the attack of the enemy.

Is there an area of your life that is the most susceptible to the enemy?

If so, what is that area?

Name one strategy for how to combat Satan in this area.

Here are some examples:

For worry and anxiety that plague the mind and rob me of God's peace, I write scripture on index cards and pray those over my situation when I feel worry creeping in.

Maybe the struggle is to speak before you think. One strategy could be to quote James 1:19, which says, "Let every man be quick to listen, slow to speak, and slow to become angry." Say it over and over in order to refrain from speaking too soon.

Now it's your turn to try.

Whatever your personal battle or struggle looks like, mentally prepare a defense. Know how you're going to combat the enemy *before* he attacks. Then look to Jesus and "set your hope fully" on Him and the grace He will provide. Then Peter basically says remember to whom we belong. We are children of God. Therefore, *act* like it! Don't conform to the old ways we used to live. Don't allow the enemy victory in areas of our lives where he used to be victorious. We are no longer ignorant children. God calls us to be holy, to be set apart, and to consecrate ourselves to Him. Why? *Because He is holy!* We are to reflect Him. He wants us to live our lives and be like Him. God wants us to open the door for Him to perform mighty works in our lives.

2. Joshua set an example to the Israelites of remembering what God had done in their lives by building an altar at Gilgal. Prior to crossing the Jordan, Joshua had already selected twelve men who represented each tribe of the nation of Israel. Those men were instructed to remove stones from the middle of the Jordan in order to set up those stones as a place of remembrance. Joshua emphasized, more than once, the need to remember what God had done for them. They didn't have the Old Testament in its entirety for every person to access and read, as we do. Nope, they relied upon passing down the stories from generation to generation. They owned their history,

they passed it down to their children, and the repetition allowed for it to seep into the marrow of their bones as truth. God did so many great things for the children of Israel. The stones at Gilgal represent the end of the wilderness pilgrimage that was the punishment for their unbelief. Gilgal represented a new beginning for them—a fresh start, so to speak. Even as they set up the stones at Gilgal, they remembered all God had done for them, how far God had brought them, and from what God had delivered them, but it also provided for them the opportunity to remember why they wandered for forty years.

How about us? Do we retell our stories of God's greatness in our lives and give Him the recognition, honor, and glory for His work? Do we tell the stories to others around us? We need to not be quiet about God's work in our lives. The more we talk about His goodness to us, the more we own that for ourselves, and it seeps into our souls and belief systems. It is much harder to forget what God has done in our lives when we continue to tell others.

Evaluate yourself for a minute.

Do you tell others of the work God is doing in your life?

If not, what keeps you from speaking up?

Sometimes we can convince ourselves that our stories aren't flashy enough to capture people's attention for Christ; we may not have a specific defining act that brings everyone to his or her knees and turns eyes toward heaven. Is it not in the journey, however, that we truly grow and our stories of God's goodness and grace unfold? In my life and in my journey, it is the faithfulness of God in the most minute details that delights me and compels me to share what God has done. If I am on a run on back roads and a deer crosses my path, I laugh out loud and know that God did that just *for me*. Those are things that delight my soul. God is amazing and faithful in the smallest areas of my life that happen on my daily journey with Him. I encourage you today to look for Him to show up in ways that are meant only for you—His little love notes to you. Then thank Him for His delights.

Day 4

Verse of the day: "Then the LORD said to Joshua, 'Today I have rolled away the reproach of Egypt from you. So the place has been called Gilgal to this day'" (Joshua 5:9).

Today we continue gleaning from Joshua's life lessons for us. Remember that yesterday we learned the importance of consecrating ourselves and remembering what God has done. Let's keep digging.

Read Joshua 5.

3. Joshua demonstrated obedience by circumcising the Jewish males according to the Law because it had ceased to be done in the wilderness (Joshua 5:2). Read Genesis 17:9–14. God established the act of circumcision as a sign of the covenant between Abraham and his descendants for generations to come. Circumcision was the outward sign of the covenant and was an act of obedience. While the Israelites wandered in the wilderness for forty years, they seemed to slip away from abiding by the covenant of circumcision. Joshua 5:4–8 explains that the children who were born on the journey out of Egypt and beyond were not circumcised. Joshua was doing what we would call some major housecleaning. So in Joshua 5, Joshua reinstituted circumcision and circumcised all the sons of Israel who had been raised up on the journey. Joshua was obedient and demonstrated the significance of obedience. They could not move forward if there was still disobedience lingering in any area. That applies to us today. Deuteronomy 30:6 says, "The LORD your God will circumcise your hearts and the hearts of your descendants, so that you may love him with all your heart and with all your soul, and you will live." Circumcise our hearts. The Hebrew word used here, *Mul*, can be used in the spiritual sense, which signifies "loyalty and obedience to God."[3] What is physical circumcision? It involves a cutting away. In our lives, we have things that we need to cut off or cut away. Circumcising our hearts involves getting rid of what is in our hearts and lives that does not honor God in order to allow our hearts to move forward in faith and obedience.

What would it look like for you to circumcise your heart?

Identify one thing you need to cut off or cut out of your life.

If you're like me, your first thought went to chocolate. I really should cut that out of my life (my waistline would thank me!), but alas, I am thankful that God gave me the gift of chocolate and do not feel convicted to rid my life of it yet.

Perhaps what needs to be cut out, however, is a nagging or recurring thought that gets you hung up and prevents you from experiencing the peace God gives. I urge you to surrender that to Him, and ask for the strength to cut whatever it is out of your life. God is faithful.

4. Joshua observed the Passover (Joshua 5:10).

It took some days for the men of Israel to heal from their recent circumcisions, so they camped and waited for a time. After the days of healing passed, the Lord told Joshua that He had "rolled away the reproach of Egypt." What did Joshua do following that? He and all of Israel observed the Passover on the fourteenth day of the month. For forty years, the Israelites had been fed from the food of heaven, from the manna God had provided. On the day following Passover, the Israelites ate from the land, and the next day the manna ceased (Joshua 5:12). This was the final indication that their wandering in the wilderness was over, and it was time for them to proceed to the new phase of their lives that God had in store for them. We must act with obedience before we see God act in our lives.

5. Joshua encountered the presence of the Lord as a direct result of his obedience to God. Look again at Joshua 5:13–15. Finally, after all these acts of obedience—the purification and the observation of the Passover—Joshua was rewarded with a visit from the commander of the Lord's army. This may have been an encounter with the preincarnate Christ. Joshua's response to this visitor was to ask if he was *for* them or *against* them. He responded that it was neither but that He'd come as commander of the Lord's army, and His message was that Joshua was standing on holy ground.

I pause here a moment because this encounter is a beautiful culmination to all Joshua had just led the children of Israel through. Sometimes we can feel so beaten down, can't we? We obey God and do what He requires of us, but it feels like we can't get ahead, no matter what we do or how obedient we are. We don't know what the outcome of our obedience will be, and we may not understand all that we are experiencing, but then God … *then* God shows up and says He sees and that we are standing on holy ground because we are rewarded with an encounter with Christ, just like Joshua. When Joshua took the reins as leader of Israel, he had quite the job duties to fulfill. And he did so with the full confidence that God was ever present. *Then* God showed up. It delights my hearts just to envision this scene and how Joshua's faith must have been fueled following that experience. It's almost as if God was saying to Joshua, "Now I can act. Now we move forward. Now is the time." But everything else had to happen first before this moment could occur.

What is it you sense that God requires of you so He can move you to the next place with Him?

Are you ready to take that next step with Him?

I urge you to be obedient when you feel God moving and stirring in your spirit. To do anything less is disobedience and will impact your journey with Him. As Joshua modeled for us, we need to consecrate, remember, circumcise our hearts, and obey His commands. Then we can encounter Christ with renewed strength and confidence in Him.

DAY 5

Verse of the day: "Then the LORD said to Joshua, 'See, I have delivered Jericho into your hands, along with its kings and its fighting men" (Joshua 6:2).

Read Joshua 6.

The time for battle and victory had finally arrived for the Israelites. They had spent many days in preparation for whatever would await them in their conquest to gain the Promised Land. (Let's be real—they had been waiting forty years for this due to the disobedience and unbelief of their fathers!) Up until this point, there had not yet been a battle. They had followed Joshua's instructions and example of obedience by preparing their hearts to trust God with the victory. Now it was time!

Jericho was on heightened alert. The city was shut up tightly (Joshua 6:1) because of their fear of the Israelites. No one was coming or going. Just imagine the tensions rising within those city walls, waiting but not knowing when exactly an attack would be.

What did God tell Joshua in Joshua 6:2?

Was this before or after the defeat of Jericho?

Isn't that just like our God? Neither the battle nor the battle strategy had been established, and God told Joshua that He had delivered Jericho into their hands. God responded to their renewed covenant with Him by granting them victory. In addition, God established to all observing nations that His presence was going with them wherever they went. Remember that Joshua was one of the initial spies whom Moses sent to scope out the land. Joshua and Caleb were the only two who returned with messages of hope and faith, stating God would provide the victory. So who better for God to use and to say *before* the battle began, "See, I have delivered

Jericho into your hands, along with its king and its fighting men." Victory was a given. Joshua just had to believe God and act in faith that God would follow through on His words.

I don't know what your life experiences are, but mine could have the potential to allow for some doubts when someone says he or she is going to do something. My immediate response is usually, "Don't tell me; show me!" The age-old saying "actions speak louder than words" rings true in my life.

Where do you fall on that spectrum? Do you tend to believe people are dependable, or do you tend to expect them to let you down?

What in your life has impacted your view of people this way?

People are human. People are going to disappoint. People are going to let us down. Some do it intentionally; some do so as a by-product of circumstances out of their control. In this world, people don't always follow through with what they say. For some of us, it is easier to trust some people's words than others'. *But God*. God is *not* like us. Praise You, Jesus. God is *always* faithful in following through with what He says. We can take Him at His word to deliver as He promises He will. God will *never* let us down. God will *never* disappoint. God will *always* do what He says. God is *always* who He says He is in scripture. Praise God, we can always count on Him. In my life, He has never let me down. That doesn't mean I always understand what He is doing or why He is doing something. That doesn't mean that He always acts in the way I want or expect Him to show up, but based upon my history with Him, I can say with confidence that I *know* He acts in my best interest.

Do you believe God acts in your best interest?

Why or why not?

Finally, God revealed His strategy for defeating Jericho. Imagine that scene. It's time for battle, and it's time to take what God has promised. But there was no battle. If you're like me, you think it's both amusing and entertaining the way God took this city for Israel. They marched around it—every day, once per day, for six days, with no shouting. Only the ark of God accompanied them, and trumpets sounded as they circled the city. Then they left. They went on back to camp until the next morning, and then they rose and did it all again. Bizarre battle strategy. *But God.* But God moves and acts in ways that are beyond our human comprehension. If you were a resident of Jericho, imagine the thoughts you would have had as you heard the trumpets as they rounded the city. Then all would be silent until the next morning. You would be wound tightly, waiting for who knows what to happen! Then day seven would arrive, and the Israelites obediently would march around the city, per God's instructions, seven times. On the seventh go-round, Joshua finally would give the command to shout. He also would include instructions regarding what was to be kept and what was to be destroyed.

In Joshua 6:17, what was to be devoted to the Lord?

Who was to be spared?

In Joshua 6:18–19, what were they to keep away from?

Why?

After that seventh march around Jericho, the walls fell down. The Israelites acted in obedience, followed Joshua's instructions, and devoted the city to the Lord. Rahab and her family were spared, as was promised. Victory was delivered into the hands of Israel, as was promised. The defeat of Jericho was sweet, and the faith of the people was strengthened that day. God provided the victory and defeat of a city on the heels of their obedience and renewed covenant. God came through. God could be trusted. Out of all of Jericho, only Rahab and her family were saved. God sees the faith of His children, and He rewards it. He wants us to trust Him to show up in mighty ways.

Is there a battleground in your life today?

Take the time here to surrender it to Jesus and to pour out your heart to Him—your fears, your doubts, and your struggles. Ask Him to help you overcome your unbelief and to trust Him to do what He says, even if it is in ways you don't understand.

Father, as we close week two, I pray that You will let the sweet victory settle over our hearts. Father, this week our confidence has been strengthened in that we know You see us, You see our hearts, and You see our acts of obedience; then You act on them. Lord God, where we struggle to surrender areas of our lives to You, I ask that You give us the courage to lay them down before You and to trust that You will provide victory in our lives. Lord, help us to consecrate ourselves to You. Help us to remember how You have acted in our lives before. Help us to circumcise our hearts before You. Help us to be obedient in areas of our lives that we might have let slip. Then we will have the precious reward of encountering Your presence in new ways. Lord, You see our hearts and know our struggles. We entrust those to You today, and we glorify and praise Your holy name. Amen.

WEEK 3

Day 1

Verse of the day: "Israel has sinned; they have violated my covenant, which I commanded them to keep. They have taken some of the devoted things; they have stolen, they have lied, they have put them with their own possessions" (Joshua 7:11).

Read Joshua 7.

Is your mind reeling after reading that chapter? Let's backpedal and read Joshua 6:27, which says, "So the LORD was with Joshua, and his fame spread throughout the land." We stopped last week with the culmination of the new covenant with Israel. They experienced a holy encounter with God, and He delivered the city of Jericho into their hands. What a spiritual high! What a renewal of faith! But ... then we open to Joshua 7:1 and read, "But the Israelites acted unfaithfully in regard to the devoted things." How did they fall so far so fast? Let's notice a couple of things in this chapter.

Remember the defeat of Jericho—wasn't it God who devised the strategy to defeat Jericho? God was the one who spoke to Joshua and told him that God was delivering Israel the victory. God then proceeded to tell Joshua how he was to go about doing that as well. As they followed God's instructions, the ark of God was also carried around the city behind the seven priests with the trumpets. Every step of the way, Joshua followed the Lord's instructions, and victory was granted.

After a quick perusal of Joshua 7:1–5, what instructions do you see are specifically from the Lord for this battle at Ai?

Did you find any?

Noticeably absent in this passage is God's instruction to spy on and attack Ai. What happened between Joshua 6 and 7? We don't know specifically, and scripture doesn't give us any insight, other than that the Israelites acted unfaithfully, and God became angry with them. Joshua, however, also got ahead of God. His victories and successes may have gotten to him a little bit, and he may have become overconfident in his own abilities, rather than acknowledging it was God working through him to achieve victory. Also, Joshua was unaware of the sin in the camp of Israel, and this also contributed to the deaths of thirty-six men and the defeat at Ai.

There is an inherent warning to us in this passage of verses. Joshua and the Israelites were on a spiritual high. God had shown up for them. His covenant with them had been renewed. God gave them victory. Somehow, they lost sight of the One who had provided the victory. Joshua didn't seek God's direction for Ai as he had with Jericho.

Isn't that just like us? We have gone through the valley, and Jesus takes us to the mountaintop with Him. We are on a spiritual high, where we feel like there is nothing God cannot do. Our faith has been renewed. Our strength and resolve has been refreshed and recharged. We feel like we are ready to tackle anything, and we may even feel like we have finally arrived at a point where we may be immune to Satan's attacks. We come down off the mountaintop with our zeal and fervor, but then we forget that it was Jesus who took us there. Somehow, we, like Joshua, don't seek His face for the next battle we encounter. It's almost as if we believe our experience on the mountaintop was all we needed, so we feel like we've got this. And we never see it coming. What was the result of that? *Defeat!* We are most vulnerable to the attacks of the enemy on the heels of a spiritual high with Jesus. The enemy doesn't like it when we are obedient to God or when we start to do His work and changes happen in our lives. The enemy of our souls gets antsy uncomfortable, and we get his attention. He turns his focus on us. Our demise becomes his priority. His ultimate goal for our lives is to *take us down*. He does not want any kingdom work to occur in our lives. *But God.* Our God is bigger. Victory will only be won when we seek God's face and confront our enemy's schemes with Jesus on our side.

Can you relate? Have you ever experienced a mountaintop moment with Christ, only to find yourself becoming confident in your own abilities and vulnerable to the attack of the enemy?

Write about it.

If not, how have you armed yourself against that vulnerability?

In our present age, we would be wise to take heed and be on guard for the tactics and schemes of the enemy. We cannot stick our heads in the sand and pretend that spiritual warfare is not present and does not impact our lives. Our culture needs us to take a stand, take up the sword, and enter the battle. Ephesians 6:12 tells us very clearly, "For our struggle is not against flesh and blood, but against the rulers, against authorities, against the powers of this dark world and *against the spiritual forces of evil in the heavenly realms*" (emphasis mine).

My sweet sister in Christ, now is the time for us to wise up to the enemy of our souls and devise a war plan that will defeat him and magnify the name of Jesus. We can't combat an enemy we can't recognize. We can't have victory without a strategy.

Are you aware of the enemy's movements in your life?

If so, how do you combat him?

Second Corinthians 10:3–5 is God's plan for victory in spiritual warfare. It says, "For though we live in the world, we do not wage war as the world does. The weapons we fight with are not the weapons of the world. On the contrary, they have the divine power to demolish strongholds. We demolish arguments and every pretension that sets itself up against the knowledge of God, and we take captive every thought to make it obedient to Christ."

If you take anything from this lesson today, I pray you take this to heart. Our enemy has already been defeated by our Jesus. He has already conquered him. The same power that raised Jesus from the dead is available to us, and He has given us that power. We can and will defeat the enemy of our souls. Don't give him an inch. We must take hold of the weapons God has placed in our arsenals and, in the name of Jesus, stand in victory in His mighty name.

Day 2

Verse of the day: "Israel has sinned; they have violated my covenant, which I commanded them to keep. They have taken some of the devoted things; they have stolen, they have lied, they have put them with their own possessions" (Joshua 7:11).

Yesterday we talked about how Joshua and Israel may have placed more weight than they should have in their own abilities and forgot to rely on God. In this same story with Achan, there is more we can learn about how our actions, whether good or bad, can have an impact on those in our spheres of influence.

In Joshua 7:11, whom did God tell Joshua had sinned?

Do you think it's fair for all of Israel to be held responsible for one man's actions?

Sometimes what we read in scripture doesn't always make sense to us—the why and the how. God's ways, however, are beyond ours, and it is our responsibility to trust Him and know that God is sovereign. The Israelites were commanded to obey the laws. God gave Joshua specific instructions regarding what was to be kept and what was to be destroyed in Jericho. There was sin in their midst, and God held them responsible as a group, rather than as individuals. God cannot abide sin—period. He could not act in their favor until they dealt with the sin that was present. Joshua responded to the defeat by tearing his clothes and falling on his face before God (see Joshua 7:6). God told him there was some hidden sin in the camp that needed to be revealed and dealt with. Joshua told the people, per the Lord's command, to again "consecrate themselves." Consecration is not a one-and-done deal. We have to continually consecrate ourselves to God and His work so He can continually act in our lives, be present in our midst, and move on our behalf. Our sins can impact those around us, and we may not even realize it. Heed the warning God has provided through the example of Achan in Joshua.

Sometimes, as much as we don't like to admit it, as believers we belong to a body.

Read 1 Corinthians 12:12–14.

How many bodies are there in Christ?

Who is part of the body of Christ?

As we see in these verses, we belong to one body in Christ. We have many different parts, but we comprise the same body. It takes all of us to function as a healthy unit for Christ. So when there is sin present in the body, the whole body suffers. In our minds, we can make justifications for our sins and that they are not hurting anyone other than ourselves (potentially—because we may not admit that our sins are hurting us). To think that our sins do not impact the body of Christ is a lie from the enemy that he wants us to believe. Not true. Think about it. When you have a stomach bug, how does the rest of your body feel? I am a runner—I love to go on runs. I don't use my stomach to run. I need my legs, feet, and knees. But if my stomach isn't well, the rest of me does not function at full capacity. Believers are called to live in unity and to hold each other accountable for the spiritual health of the body and for the spiritual health of you and me individually.

Name an example of how the sin of one individual can impact the growth and spiritual health of the group.

Achan could not resist the allure of the "beautiful robe from Babylonia, two hundred shekels of silver, and a wedge of gold, weighing fifty shekels" (Joshua 7:21). Just imagine how far that much silver and gold would go back in those days. Achan said he saw it and then he "coveted" it. He wanted it. He desired it. He had to have it. God very specifically instructed the people of Israel to destroy the devoted things. Achan still disobeyed. His disobedience cost Israel the lives of thirty-six of their men. God's punishment was swift and direct. Achan and all of his belongings, his sons, and his daughters were taken to the Valley of Achor, stoned, and then burned. A memorial was made in that place as a reminder of the high stakes of being unfaithful and disobedient to God.

God is a holy God, and He cannot tolerate sin in His presence because it is the antithesis of His nature. As believers, we cannot expect our relationships with God to grow and flourish when there is hidden sin or when we're holding on to something secret in our lives. It may not seem to be that big of a deal, and we may have allowed ourselves to make minor concessions. But hear me: little concessions to sin become big concessions to sin. Where does that leave our relationships with Christ? With unconfessed or hidden sins in our lives, our relationships with God cannot move forward. We have a broken connection with God when we purposefully continue to hide or carry around sin in our lives. God is holy. He desires us to be holy like Him. Not only does he desire us to be holy, but He also *commands* us to be holy like Him. When we begin to allow what we would call the "little sins" to creep in, we are placing ourselves at risk for all kinds of sins to enter our lives. We are inviting sin into our lives. Our intimacy with Christ suffers. Then the enemy has victory, and we feel defeated. *But God.* Praise Jesus, He says, "If we confess them to Him, He is faithful and just to forgive us our sins, and to cleans us from all unrighteousness" (1 John 1:9). It was only after Achan's punishment was meted out that the Lord's anger turned away from the children of Israel. They had to deal with the sin problem in their midst before His anger left them.

Is there a hidden sin or a minor concession you are making in your life?

If so, write it here.

Are you willing to confess it and surrender it to God today? Remember that He delights in giving us victory in our efforts to please Him. He will not disappoint or let you down.

Write a prayer of confession and thanksgiving for all that God is doing in your life today.

Day 3

Verse of the Day: "And patience is better than pride" (Ecclesiastes 7:8b).

As I read about what Israel experienced in their conquest of the Promised Land—I'm not going to lie—I felt emotionally exhausted and spent, thinking about all of their ups and downs, their victories, and their defeats. I even got frustrated with them as I read through their journeys because, to me, it seems so obvious what they were missing when they messed up. At times, that frustration can take on a little bit of judgment in their lack of long-term memory—how quickly they seem to forget all God has done for them and go right back to their former way of thinking. Granted, they improved a lot in that area from the wilderness wanderings. The steps of purification and consecration that Joshua directed them did seem to make their faith and renewed covenant with God more authentic. They didn't, as a group, steal the plunder and hide it.

They were punished as a group because there was sin in the camp, and God could not move or act with that in their midst. I like to keep a running dialogue with God as I read His Word, and more than once, I've said to Him, "Why couldn't they see what they were doing? Why did they continue to repeat the cycle of unbelief, Your action, then belief? Would it not have been so much easier to just continue to believe?" Think about *all* of the miracles they saw as they wandered in the wilderness. Think about the countless ways God acted in their lives. He literally provided them food from heaven, for goodness sake. He brought water from a rock. He parted the sea for them to cross on dry land—*dry land*. Then they grumbled and complained. Fast-forward to their children entering the Promised Land. These were the children born during the wandering years, so they witnessed God's provision at some point. The Israelites also passed down their stories and history by retelling through the generations, so they would not be forgotten. Some of them who were children in the wilderness may have even felt like I feel when I read about their expedition.

So in Joshua and the Promised Land, we see less of that. However, we did just see yesterday that after the victory in Jericho, they seemed to not seek the face of God as they moved forward. And *bam*! That frustration I used to feel creeps back in. *But God.* He, with a gentle reminder and His Holy Spirit, reminded me or impressed upon me (okay, maybe even convicted me) this question: "Dawn, have you, at times, not done the exact same thing to me?" *Whoa! Yes, Lord, yes, yes, yes, I have. I can't make a justification with that one.*

It was about that time that my knees hit the floor in confession and repentance, and I begged for humility and grace. Countless times, over the years, God has given me a particular image when I make a choice that is inconsistent with His Word—the image of me throwing back in Jesus's face what He did for me on the cross. Then I am humbled. When I sin, whatever that sin may be, that is exactly what I am doing. I am saying to Christ, "I know that You died on the cross, and I am choosing to hang You back on that cross again with the choice I am making." *Ouch!* Thank You, Father, for the convicting and subsequent cleansing of the Holy Spirit.

Can you think of a time when you threw back in the face of Christ what He did for you on the cross?

If so, what was it?

How will that image impact you in the future when faced with submitting to a temptation or choosing to be obedient?

Here we are after the stoning of Achan and his family, and God tells Joshua to not be afraid or discouraged. Don't you just love that about God? He is just and has to discipline His children in order to grow us and mature us in Him. But He knows that His discipline can make us feel discouraged that we can't get it right, and He, in His loving manner, says to not be discouraged. So after the Israelites took care of their sin problem, God moved them forward. He provided them with hope and courage.

Read Joshua 8.

What a difference it makes to wait on the Lord, right? Praise Jesus for His countless examples in scripture that offer us hope and instruction. His Word provides so much guidance and speaks truth into our everyday experiences. God provided the instruction and battle strategy for the Israelites to have victory over Ai this time. The army of Israel was obedient to God's commands and Joshua's instruction. They ambushed the army of Ai and were victorious. Joshua held out his javelin until all was destroyed in Ai (see Joshua 8:18, 26). In Jericho, the Israelites were told to destroy everything; whatever could not be destroyed or burned up was placed in the treasury of the Lord (Joshua 6:24). However, unlike in Jericho, the Israelites were allowed to carry off plunder from the city of Ai. It just makes me stop and think: if only Achan had not been so greedy or had been patient and waited on the Lord, he could have taken livestock and plunder with God's blessing.

How many if-only moments can you recall from your own life? We usually only say this after the fact—after we had to learn a lesson the hard way. Why must we make our lives more complicated than they have to be? Sometimes I envision God sitting there, shaking His head at our stubbornness and occasionally thinking with affection, *Humans!* We just don't get it, do we? God has clearly said in His Word that we are to wait on Him. We are an instantaneous society and culture. We want what we want and cannot bear to wait for anything! I have found myself getting frustrated over waiting for insignificant things. Our instant gratification mind-set has nearly eradicated our appreciation of waiting on things. We miss some of the greatest lessons of life because we cannot wait for anything.

Patience with circumstances and patience with people are both addressed at length in the New Testament. David discussed waiting on the Lord repeatedly in the psalms. I challenge you to read through the New Testament and take note of all the times we are encouraged to be patient. Our lack of patience has caused many of us heartbreak that cannot be undone. Thankfully, God is gracious and full of mercy, love, and compassion. He gives us hope and healing. Praise God for His goodness. He truly does make things work out for our good. What blessing may we have missed, though, had we only been patient from the beginning?

Do you have any if-only experiences in your life?

What do you wish you had done differently?

How have you seen God work through that situation anyway?

Has your ability to wait on the Lord matured since that time?

Isaiah 30:18 says, "Yet the LORD longs to be gracious to you; he rises to show you compassion. For the Lord is a God of justice. Blessed are all who wait for him." Psalm 27:14 says, "Wait for the LORD; be strong and take heart, and wait for the LORD." God wants us to wait for Him. We may not always understand for what we are waiting, but there are times in our spirits when we know we must wait. Other times, we want an immediate answer to a question—college choice, career, where to live, who to marry—and God may not give us an immediate answer. The blessing comes with the waiting. He will always show us His will when we earnestly seek His face and pursue Him.

Day 4

Verse of the day: "Afterward Joshua read all the words of the law—the blessings and the curses—just as it is written in the Book of the Law" (Joshua 8:34).

This portion of scripture feels so precious to me.

Read Joshua 8:30–35.

Following their conquest of Ai, Joshua built an altar. They offered a burnt offering and fellowship offerings on this altar. What is a fellowship offering, you may ask? That was my question too. A fellowship offering is the Hebrew word *Selem*.[4] which specifies which portions of an animal are sacrificed, and the meat is shared with the priest. Leviticus 7:12–17 describes the fellowship offering. It can be offered as "an expression of thankfulness" or a result of a vow. According to the Hebrew definition, some scholars believe it "typified the worshiper's feeling of peace with God." We don't really know what the purpose of this offering is in Joshua. It very well could be a combination of all of the above. Regardless, it seems to denote thankfulness. Clearly, the Israelites have much for which to be thankful. God delivered them from their wilderness wanderings. He provided defeats in Jericho and Ai. He revealed to them sin in their midst so they could purify themselves as a people group. In the second conquest, he provided them with livestock and plunder. So they offered Him fellowship offerings and burnt offerings.

Then Joshua copied on stones the Law of Moses, and he read all of it to them. They did not have the luxury of owning their own Bibles or even the Pentateuch, which is the first five books of the Old Testament. They needed someone to read it to them. Doesn't that make you take a step back and thank God for His goodness to us that we live in a country in which Bibles are easily accessible to us, and we can pick which version we want? As I write this, I'm sitting with three different Bible versions. Do we take for granted our access to His Word? Who cares how many Bibles we have if we don't take the time to open them and hear what God has to say to us?

Do you believe God continues to speak through His Word?

How often do you dig into the scriptures to hear what He has to say?

Joshua 8:35 is so precious to me, and I read it with such tenderness. It says, "There was not a word of all that Moses had commanded that Joshua did not read to the whole assembly of Israel, *including the women and children, and the aliens who lived among them*" (emphasis mine).

Two things are here that just make my heart full. The women and children sat among them to hear the spoken word. Make no mistake—God uses women *and* children in His work and values them as treasured jewels, just as He does men. Never think that God doesn't have a place for you in His work or in His church because of your age or your gender. God is so awesome like that!

Joshua 8:35 very clearly refers to the aliens who lived among the children of Israel. Aliens were those who weren't Jewish. Rahab and all of her family lived among them. God made Himself known even to them. First Peter 2:11 says this: "Dear friends, I urge you, as aliens and strangers in the world, to abstain from sinful desires which war against your soul." The term *aliens* in Joshua refers to those who did not belong to the tribes of Israel but chose to live among them. Interestingly enough, the Israelites were the ones who were often the aliens in the lands through which they journeyed, going back to Abraham. Then, the New Testament tells us that we are aliens and strangers in *this world*. The Greek word for aliens is *Paroikos*, which is defined as "a sojourner, a temporary dweller not having settled home in the place where he currently resides."[5] This is not your final destination. Don't get comfortable!! There are so many things in this world that pull at us, that tempt us, that tell us to focus on the right now.

What messages do we see surrounding us everywhere we go? Our culture bombards us with the message that it's all about us—that we should do what makes us happy, live for the moment, and there is no absolute truth. Listen to me: that is not what the Bible says. In fact, what does 1 Peter say? It says to abstain from the sinful desires. Abstain doesn't mean to partake just a little bit. No, it means *stay away*. Have no part of it! I am so thankful that this world is not my home. My true home is with Jesus, the city whose maker is the Lord. That is my home. How easily it becomes to be settled here where we reside and to lose sight of the ultimate goal and prize. We sometimes want to be comfortable here. As a Christian on this earth, I never truly feel like I belong because my heart yearns for Jesus.

Do you live in such a way that says this earth is not your permanent home?

In what ways have you become settled where you currently are?

What cultural messages about the here-and-now have you internalized?

Read Acts 2:42–47.

Acts 2:42 says, "They devoted themselves to the apostles' teaching and to the fellowship, to the breaking of bread, and to prayer." They met together. They shared meals together. They shared life together. They prayed together. They opened their homes to each other. This passage of scripture is where most churches refer for small-group ministry. On the heels of our talking about living as aliens here on earth, and this earth not being our home, this passage of scripture shows us where we can find true community while living as aliens here. Our fellow believers in Christ are strangers with us on the journey. Together, we can share life and have a place of belonging while we wait for our true home. For some of us, that's easier than for others. Our nature or defense mechanism can be to isolate or to protect ourselves from such intimacy with others. *But God.* He created us for fellowship. He created us for relationships. We are relational beings, created in the image of our God. It is challenging to adhere to the urgent command in 1 Peter to live as aliens and to abstain from sinful desires. On our own, that difficulty is multiplied. How easy is it to shoot a quick text when you're struggling, asking a friend or mentor in the faith for prayer? Accountability is what we have among one another in community that helps us to live by God's standards.

On a scale of one to ten, rate yourself on how well you are living as an alien and stranger on earth, with one being that you need to make some changes and ten reflecting you've arrived.

What changes do you need to make in your life to make it a point to live differently?

Life is not easy. God did not intend for us to live life on our own. I encourage you to share with those closest to you where you struggle to be different so you can hold one another accountable. I encourage you to join a small group or find a Bible study in which you can immerse yourself if you don't already have a group of people as your community as you journey through your time on earth as a stranger. Be thoughtful as you go through your day today, noting where you see yourself living as an alien and abstaining from sinful desires. Ask God to give you insight and strength. Blessings to you on your journey!

DAY 5

Verse of the day: "But all the leaders answered, 'We have given them our oath by the LORD, the God of Israel, and we cannot touch them now'" (Joshua 9:19).

The victories God granted the children of Israel had become widespread knowledge. You can bet that the neighboring countries were getting a bit antsy, to say the least. So what did they do? Rather than go to war against them, they devised a deceptive plan—to deceive them into a covenant in order to live.

Read Joshua 9:1–15.

Was there anything in this passage that stuck out for you?

If so, what and why?

My thoughts immediately go to verse 14, where the men of Israel sample the provisions of the men but once again, they "did not inquire of the LORD" (Joshua 9:14). Did we not see them learn their lesson the hard way? Earlier in the week, we noted how the children of Israel experienced defeat in Ai and lost some of their men as a result of not seeking the guidance and direction of the Lord first. Here they go again! Stubborn, right? Isn't that just like us, though? There are some things in our lives for which we are stubborn so that it takes us several attempts before we ever learn the lesson we need to learn.

Can you think of an example from your own life?

If so, what lesson did it take you a few attempts to learn?

In addition, we may think we have already learned the lesson, and what do we do? We grow confident in our own abilities and may forget to seek the face of Jesus for continual strength and support to sustain the lessons learned in our lives. Thus, we put ourselves at risk of having to learn the lesson all over again. In Joshua 9, after having tasted of the samples, Joshua made an oath with the Hivites, a "treaty of peace," without ever asking the Lord what to do. Interesting to note here, though, is that when Joshua was talking to the Gibeonites, they recounted to him all they had heard God had done for them. When God acts in our lives, His fame cannot be kept quiet. We should want to shout from the rooftops what He has done for us. We cannot keep God and His resurrecting power a secret in our lives.

Read Joshua 9:16–26 to see what happens when they discover the deception.

What, if anything, about this passage, surprises you?

In spite of the deception, Joshua kept the oath of protection that the leaders of Israel made with the Gibeonite people. An oath or covenant was a very serious thing. It was something into which one did not enter lightly, even if it was made under false pretenses. The children of Israel were not too happy about it, but Joshua would not let them harm the Gibeonites. When Joshua inquired of them what the reason was for their deceit, they answered honestly that they feared for their lives because they'd heard that God had commanded Moses to wipe out all the inhabitants of the land. Joshua kept the oath made to them and made them servants. However, their place of service was at the altar of the Lord. There's access and opportunity to learn about the one true God!!

Just like Joshua, our words should mean something, and the power in them should not be taken lightly. When we say we will do something, we should follow through with what we say. We should take care with our words as well. They have the power to lift up and the power to tear down. Words can wound and destroy or heal and encourage, depending on what we choose to do with them.

James 3 talks about the power of the tongue and how deadly it can be. James 3 also warns us against the challenge of taming our tongues. "But no man can tame the tongue. It is a restless evil, full of deadly poison" (James 3:8). We must be on guard about the words that come out of our mouths, which is strictly overflow from what is building up in our hearts. Whoa! Does that make you stop right there and do a self-check? It stops me! With that warning blaring in my ears, it makes me take a humble step backward.

Ephesians 4:29 tells us this: "Let no unwholesome talk come out of your mouths, but only what is helpful for building others up according to their needs, that it may benefit those who listen." Did your mama ever tell you, "If you don't have something nice to say, then don't say anything at all"? Well, that is rooted right there in Ephesians 4:29. Say what benefits others, what meets their needs, and what will encourage them. That doesn't mean to be fake or insincere. Just watch your words!

Colossians 4:6 states, "Let your conversation be always full of grace, seasoned with salt, so that you may know how to answer everyone." Full of grace! One foolproof way to keep your tongue in check, based upon this verse, is to remind yourself what God's grace has meant to you and done for you.

Over and over again in scripture, we read about guarding our tongues and our words and how they impact so much of our lives and the world around us. I challenge you to go one full day, saying *only* what you mean, what is true, what is seasoned with salt, what is full of grace, what will encourage, and what is wholesome. See how it changes your entire day and your mood! Are you up to the challenge?

Do you feel the Holy Spirit pinpointing an area of your speech in which you need to allow God's grace to pour down?

If so, what is it, and how can you make an effort to change it?

Offer your petitions to the Father here.

Precious, beautiful Savior, thank You for giving us Your Word and allowing us to experience the power and presence of Your Holy Spirit at work in our lives. Lord, there are so many lessons that we can learn from the pages of Joshua that apply to our lives today. Help us to continue to look to You for guidance and provision. Test our hearts and reveal to us the areas of our lives in which we need to turn our tongues and our hearts over to You. Lord, if we are withholding anything from You, I beg of You to show us so that You can continue to pour out into our lives. Help us, Lord, to walk in full obedience and complete surrender to You. You bless our lives in countless ways, and we praise You today!

WEEK 4

Day 1

Verse of the day: "The Gibeonites then sent word to Joshua in the camp at Gilgal: 'Do not abandon your servants. Come up to us quickly and save us! Help us because the Amorite kings from the hill country have joined forces against us'" (Joshua 10:6).

Let's check in with Joshua to see what is going on his world—and what it means for you and me!

Read Joshua 10:1–8.

Remember back to last week. The Gibeonites deceived Joshua and the leaders of Israel into making a covenant of peace with them. Even after the deception was revealed, the Israelites were bound by it. We emphasized the importance of our words—their impact and effects. It didn't seem to take too long before Israel was called on to make good on their word. Other kings got nervous and felt threatened as they observed and heard what was going on with Israel. Israel destroyed Jericho and then Ai. Then they entered into a peace treaty with Gibeon, so five other kings joined forces together and devised a plan to attack Gibeon because of that treaty. If ever there was a time to test the strength of that treaty, it was right then.

The Gibeonites were able to get word to Joshua that they were being attacked, and they basically reminded Joshua of their covenant. Look at the word choice: "Do not abandon your servants. Come up to us quickly and save us! Help us, because all the Amorite kings from the hill country have joined forces against us" (Joshua 10:6). When I read those words, I hear some pleading desperation. They didn't say, "Come join us in the battle, if you so choose. We are stronger together than apart."

No, they basically said to remember we are your servants and please *save us!* They had faith in Joshua and the power of God that accompanied him and Israel. They believed that Joshua would make good on his word and show up. When I read their plea to him, I do not see it laced with doubt as they asked for help. And they were not disappointed. Joshua wasted no time in gathering his forces and marching to the aid of the Gibeonites. Joshua and his men showed up in the power of the Lord! Are we like the Gibeonites when we pray and ask God to show up for us? Every day we have the opportunity to choose whether or not we are going to believe God and trust in His ability to follow through.

Do you pray with confidence in the One to whom you are praying?

How do you react when God's response does not align with what you are hoping to receive?

Colossians 4:2 says, "Devote yourselves to prayer, being watchful and thankful." From there, Paul goes one step further and asks them to pray for him and his missionary team as well. What does a life devoted to prayer look like? I can remember times in my walk with Christ when fellow believers would use phrases like "devote yourselves to prayer" or other similar statements, and I would think, *Yes, okay, I hear you. But what does that mean?* I am a get-down-to-the-nitty-gritty kind of girl. I want to understand what something means and how to live that out. So back to the verse in Colossians—devote yourselves to prayer. How can we devote ourselves to prayer? This is the question before us. If you're like me, you don't have the ability to spend all day in a prayer closet. We all have responsibilities—families, jobs, homes to maintain, church, small groups, a plethora of other commitments—and these things require our time and our attention. We cannot neglect these things, nor should we. Devoting ourselves to prayer is an attitude of the heart that includes committed times of focused attention to our prayer lives.

When faced with a challenge, what is your go-to response? Does your heart immediately bow in the posture of humility and ask God to help you through? When faced with a decision, is your response to fret, worry, and let your mind race, or is it to take it before the throne of grace and ask for God's wisdom and direction? These responses don't immediately occur; they are cultivated as part of a relationship—an outpouring of a passionate prayer life and dependence on God. Prayer is one key component of how we communicate with God and our relationship with Him. Countless times I have heard someone say, in reference to prayer, "How do you know someone if you never talk to him?" And it is so true. How will we ever learn to hear what the Father's voice sounds like if we never seek Him and pursue Him in prayer?

I came to know Christ as a young girl in my home church in southern Georgia. My relationship with Jesus has been quite the journey. I chose to be selfish and did what I wanted more times than I like to admit. I turned my back on my relationship with God for a period of years in which my heart was broken, and I returned as the prodigal daughter, knowing that my only true contentment and satisfaction in this life was found in Jesus Christ. But at the same time, I didn't know how to return to Him with all the guilt and shame I carried. Day by day, He showed me how to release it back to Him and let His mercy, grace, compassion, love, and forgiveness pour out over my life. Yet at the beginning, I wasn't sure how to regain that communication with Him. I used to talk so freely to Him and pour out my heart to Him. I understood the verse in 1 Thessalonians that said to pray without ceasing. I would have an ongoing dialogue with Jesus throughout my day ... and then I fell prey to the enemy and, in my heart, felt I had lost all of that.

I'm not saying I lost my salvation because I knew my eternal state was secure before God, but I had made choices that put me at odds with God. I would cry out in frustration upon my return to Christ because I wanted that intimacy with God to return and didn't know how to make it. What I realized, as time went on, was that it took the cultivation of my daily prayer life to return to that state, praise Jesus. My prayer life didn't return to a previous state. No, God is beyond merciful and full of grace, and He has taken it to a whole new level of intimacy and beauty with Him, and I am humbled by it daily. Thank You, Jesus.

How would you describe your prayer life?

Where do you struggle the most when you pray? For example, does your mind race and your thoughts shoot off in multiple directions? Or do you find yourself not knowing how to begin or what to say?

Don't be discouraged if you feel like you are struggling with prayer today. Take heart! Every transition begins with a single decision, a single step. God doesn't require fancy words or long dissertations in prayer. He wants our honesty, our vulnerability, our willingness, and our desire to pursue a relationship with Him in passionate prayer. That's all! God is faithful, and He will meet us where we are—and for each one of us, that place is different. Begin today by writing a prayer of thankfulness and renewed dedication to pursuing Him in prayer.

Day 2

Verse of the day: "The LORD said to Joshua, 'Do not be afraid of them; I have given them into your hand. No one will be able to withstand you" (Joshua 10:8).

Guaranteed victory! Hang on to that little phrase, and let it saturate to the core of your soul. Reread yesterday's verse of the day, and then read today's again. There was no hesitation on Joshua's part to rally his troops and rush to the aid of the Gibeonites. Before the battle had even begun for the Israelites, the Lord told Joshua not to fear because he would have victory. That's some confidence going into battle—no worries because it's already won. Guaranteed victory!

If you were to take an inventory of your life, where would the phrase "guaranteed victory" or the truth of that mean the most for you? In other words, where do you need guaranteed victory in your life?

Read Joshua 10:7–15.

Prior to the battle, Joshua knew it was theirs for the taking. However, it was not without much effort on their part. They still had to fight and do what they did in order to win. Rarely is a battle fought without any energy expenditure, even when it is a guaranteed victory. Oftentimes, it is in the battle that we experience growth in our lives. Then the victory becomes that much sweeter, and our faith in God grows. We mature spiritually, and God is glorified. Did you happen to notice in Joshua 10:9 that it was after an all-night march that the Israelites entered the battle? To me, this means they already lost a night of sleep and could have felt a little tired already. I don't know about you, but girlfriend needs her some sleep! To have to enter a battle tired would not make for a very good soldier right here. Thank God for His faithfulness and sustaining strength. In addition to the guaranteed victory that was promised to Israel on this day, they also witnessed their very own miracle. Joshua prayed that the sun would stand still and that the moon would stop until Israel had "avenged itself on its enemies" (Joshua 10;13).

Whoa! It says it delayed going down for a full day. Just take a minute and envision this scene. Israel has marched all night. They then engaged in a battle that had to feel like it was never going to end … because the sun stood still until their victory was triumphed. Imagine the physical exhaustion they had to have felt. *But God.* But God sustained them, and they were able to endure because they *knew* that victory was theirs for the taking. As I sit at my desk typing this, I want to clap my hands for the glory of the Lord. Does He ever just awe you with His complete amazing-ness?

Sometimes, it can feel like the God of the Old Testament doesn't quite move in the same way in our lives. Yet when we feel that way, we sell God short, and, ultimately, it is a sin of unbelief. Hebrews 13:8 says, "Jesus Christ is the same yesterday and today and forever." Take heart, dear sister in Christ! Jesus is the same. That same God who made the sun stand still and the moon stop turning is your Jesus and my Jesus. We don't open our hearts in belief wide enough to allow God the freedom to work and move in our lives as He wants to do. We keep His movement in our lives stifled with limitations we place on Him with our unbelief. First Corinthians 2:9 states, "No eye has seen, no ear has heard, no mind has conceived what God has prepared for those who love Him." We cannot even begin to fathom what God is capable of in our lives because we limit Him. Why did the Israelites have such a great victory? Because they took God at His word and stepped forward in faith that He had given them the battle—their responsibility was only to believe Him and fight the fight. We can have that same victory in our lives—in any and every area! Where do you need guaranteed victory? Is God pressing upon your heart to do something, but you're unsure of the outcome so you hold back—you put limits on Him? Is God saying, "Trust Me enough to let go of _____"? (Fill in the blank!) Maybe it's something that is less tangible and harder to articulate. Whatever it is, God does not want His daughters to live in defeat. Listen to me; Satan loves nothing better than to kick us down and have us believe that God couldn't possibly give us victory in whatever our areas of need are. He is the father of lies, and he laughs at you when you buy into his baloney. The Jesus of the Bible—my Jesus, *your* Jesus—gives us victory. First John 5:4 informs us that our faith is the victory that has overcome the world. It tells us that everyone born of God overcomes the world. We have the power of Christ in us to give us victory. We are not to be held in a cycle of defeat. "It is for freedom that Christ has set us free" (Galatians 5:1).

Read Ephesians 1:19–20.

Jesus Christ died on the cross, was buried, and rose again three days later. The very same power that raised Jesus from the dead and seated Him at the right hand of His Father *is the power at work in you and me.* We have access to this power through the blood of Jesus. The power of Christ is far greater than the power of death and the enemy.

Where do you need a refill of the power of Christ in your life?

What has held you back from claiming that power of the Holy Spirit as your right as a child of God?

The Bible does not promise that victory will come easily for us. Look at the example in Joshua. They fought all day—for an extended day, unlike any other in history—after being up all night, marching. But God had guaranteed their victory. They believed Him. They fought. They were victorious. As a result, faith was increased, and God was glorified. Amen!

Don't give up, precious daughter of God. The end of your battle may be nowhere in sight. In fact, your battle may only be beginning. *But God.* But God has this. He goes before you and behind you. When you step out in faith and obedience to Him, He will give you victory over your enemy. He sees you fighting. He will sustain you with His strength. He delights in you as a beloved child. Sense His closeness to you today, and rest in it. I love being in His Word with you. Bless you. Thank You, Jesus.

Day 3

Verse of the day: "Do not be afraid; do not be discouraged. Be strong and courageous. This is what the LORD will do to all the enemies you are going to fight" (Joshua 10:25).

Read Joshua 10:16–28.

Claiming the Promised Land was no small task. The Israelites were to take possession of the land, but the land was already occupied. So this possession included numerous bloody battles. In the passage we just read, Joshua and his army were in hot pursuit of the five kings, who had fled and hid in caves. We read that Joshua and his army destroyed completely the cities of these kings. Tuck away the term "completely" as it pertains to the extent of the destroying that Joshua was instructed to do. They rolled a stone in front of the kings' hiding place and guarded it while destroying all of the kings' men. After this victory, Joshua wanted the stone of the cave rolled back in order to deal with the five kings. Let's take a minute and consider this—the kings ran and hid while their men were fighting for their lives, their families, their homes, and their cities. Is that the kind of king you want to serve—the kind who takes off when the heat of the battle is at its greatest? A hiding king is the equivalent of a cowardly king. Praise God that our King of kings did not run and hide when He was pursued by His enemies. No, our King willingly allowed Himself to be captured, tortured, mocked, ridiculed, beaten, and crucified on a cross in order to save His people. That's what a true king does. Thank You, Lord Jesus, for being the King who gave His life for me. And our King is returning for us one day. Praise You, Jesus!

Back to the cowardly kings in Joshua—yes, that's what we shall call them moving forward. Joshua had the cowardly kings brought to him and called all of the army of Israel to join him. In Joshua 10:24, Joshua tells the men, "Come here and put your feet on the necks of these kings." That was a symbolic gesture of "victory and promised assurance of future conquest."[6]

What did we talk about yesterday? That guaranteed victory! Notice God's consistency. Doesn't His consistency provide you with peace of mind? Our relationships with Him aren't like some of our human relationships can be. We don't have to wonder what we're going to get with God today when we roll out of bed in the morning. We don't have to wonder what mood He will be in today. We don't have to wonder if we have made Him angry. We don't have to be insecure in our standing with Him. We don't have to wonder if we have a place of belonging with Him. We don't have to wonder if God's promises are the same day by day. No, we can trust and rest in God's consistency—in His character, love, friendship, holiness, grace, and goodness.

What part of the consistency of God means the most to you at this point in your life?

Why do you believe that is so?

What part of God's consistency is a struggle for you to trust?

Pause a moment and tell Him about it. Ask for the ability to trust that part of who He is.

Reread our verse of the day. Is this the first time we have read the words, "Do not be afraid. Do not be discouraged. Be strong and courageous"? Nope! It is not! Multiple times we have read that the Lord say to Joshua to be strong and courageous, and don't be afraid. How awesome it is to see Joshua take God at His word, internalize it, and then pass those same words of comfort to the Israelites. We can't speak truth to people in our lives if we don't believe it ourselves. The words we share must be spoken from a place of authenticity. How can I tell someone to not be afraid and to believe God when I myself cannot believe God is true to His word? Do you believe a person more for what she says or for what she does? We can say what we believe all day long. But the rubber meets the road in what we are doing. We make choices in our lives and behave in ways that reflect our true belief systems.

Evaluate yourself. What would you say your behaviors and choices reflect about your belief system?

Are they in alignment with what you say you believe?

These are tough heart questions. Authenticity before God is imperative. It is critical. It should be our hearts' desire. When we are authentic before God, He empowers us and enables us to be authentic in life. Who we are before Almighty God is the only thing that truly matters in the grand scheme of this life. Don't you think there was a reason that God told Joshua over and over to not be afraid? Joshua must have been fearful for God to have told him not to fear. God knew and saw Joshua's heart—his authentic self—and spoke truth right into it. Joshua must have felt discouragement because God told him to not be discouraged. It's okay; it is *safe* to be our authentic selves to God. God didn't judge or condemn Joshua for his fear and discouragement. God wanted only to get to the heart of the matter and breathe His truth into Joshua's life. It is the same way for us. God doesn't want us to wait until we feel like we are "good enough" in our own minds to present ourselves before Him. No, He wants us to approach Him in the midst of our flaws, our fears, our failures, our hopes, and our dreams and present ourselves to Him just as we are. Then He can lift our heads and our hope, and let us rest in who we are in Him.

Thank You, Lord Jesus, for loving us as we are and giving us the freedom to be authentic before You so that we can be authentic in life. As we journey through this day and all that You have planned for us, help us to look for You every step of the way and to follow where You lead. Help us to not get caught up in our own insecurities and then cease to be authentic in our lives. Lord, help us to know and to trust that we are safe with You and that we need not fear or be discouraged. Help us follow the example of Joshua today. In Your most holy and precious name, amen.

Day 4

Verse of the day: "So Joshua took the entire land, just as the LORD had directed Moses, and He gave it as an inheritance to Israel according to their tribal divisions. Then the land had rest from war" (Joshua 11:23).

Read Joshua 10:29–11:23.

This passage outlines the conquests of Israel in taking over the land that God had promised to them. Repeatedly in these verses, we see the total conquest of kings and cities. This onslaught took approximately seven years.[7] Joshua was not exactly young when these battles began—remember he was one of the original spies Moses sent out to scope the land *prior* to the Israelites wandering in the wilderness. He was of age then. For the next forty years, he wandered in the wilderness. According to one commentary, Joshua was nearly ninety years old around the time he followed in Moses's footsteps. Never let age be a deterrent to what God can and wants to do through you.

Kings and cities were dethroned and destroyed in order for Israel to claim what God had given to them. Not only did the cities have to be destroyed but also the ruler of the cities. Think about it—if the city had been destroyed but the king was still intact, then the battle would have only been temporarily and partially won because the land still belonged to the king, even if he didn't have anyone in his kingdom.

The same thought and principle can apply to our lives too. Partial obedience always comes back to haunt us. The king was the ruler, the one authority to whom the people submitted. Take a look at your life.

What would you say rules or controls your life?

To what or whom do you submit yourself?

Perhaps a different question is, what or whom do you hold in a place of high prominence in your life that you allow to affect and determine your decisions?

Would you consider this an idol?

According to *Webster's Dictionary*, an idol is defined as "a representation or symbol of an object of worship."[8] An idol is something that is worshiped. It is placed in a position of high esteem. It has prominence and value in our lives. The Old Testament is full of examples of God telling His children to tear down the high places. Over and over in the chronicles of the kings of Israel, we see them setting up the high places for themselves or the Lord saying they did not tear down the high places. At times, kings were mentioned, and it was noted that they did indeed tear down the high places. What is the big deal, you might ask, if they did not fully eradicate the high places? There is no room on the throne of your heart for more than one King, and He will not share that position. Therefore, we daily make a choice of who or what we place on that throne. When we refuse to tear down the idols in our lives, we cannot live in the fullness and complete satisfaction in our relationships with Christ.

Exodus 34:13–14 tells us this: "Break down their altars, smash their sacred stones and cut down their Asherah poles. Do not worship any other god, for the LORD whose name is Jealous, is a jealous God." Our God is a jealous God. Our God loves us so much and so desires a relationship with us that He is indeed *jealous* for our worship and desire. In 1 Corinthians 10:14, we read this: "Therefore, my dear friends, flee from idolatry." This verse falls right in the middle of Paul's warnings that can be learned from the history of Israel.

What are the consequences of leaving some of those high places? They are countless and have the potential to be devastating, both to us and to our families. First and foremost, the most devastating effect by far of placing something other than Jesus on the throne of our hearts is that it creates a divide in our relationships with Him. In order for my life to be satisfying and for me to have any purpose, I must be in the center of God's will. I must not allow anything to block my communication with Him. That communication with the Father is imperative to the condition of my soul and spirit. Without it, I am as lost as a ship without a rudder. I have no aim, no purpose, no direction. Never mind the times when I am seeking to make a life decision and want to hear what God wants me to do. If I have pursued other things ahead of Him, when the going gets tough and I need Him, I then will be far away from Him.

So then this breakdown in communication impacts our ability to make decisions that God desires and that honor Him. It is a domino effect. The further we drift, the worse it becomes for us, and the easier it becomes to place something else in God's rightful place. Jesus paid the penalty of my sins on the cross of Calvary. He *deserves* my life lived in full surrender and submission to Him. He *belongs* on the throne of my heart and your heart.

Earlier in the study we discussed how making concessions in small things opens the door to making concessions in bigger things. It is no truer than right here, when we make small concessions that place something else as the king of our lives. When we do that, we have created an idol.

How do we determine if something is an idol? Ask yourself the following questions, and be honest with your answers. Ask God to reveal to you things you may need to see.

How do I spend my time?

Do I set aside time daily to spend in the presence of God?

When life gets busy, what is the first thing that I let slide?

What impacts and influences my decisions?

What do I talk about with other people?

Am I harboring little pockets of unforgiveness in my heart?

Am I harboring little pockets of jealousy in my heart?

Am I harboring ill feelings toward other people, and my heart is beginning to harden?

What makes me feel happy and content?

What satisfies me?

What am I passionate about?

Have I invited God into all of the areas of my life and asked Him to take over and be glorified in all of my activities, conversations, and relationships?

How do I spend my money?

Who are my closest friends?

Do they share the same passions and values for Christ as I do?

Am I the same person in all areas of my life?

What do I think about?

What are my life goals?

How do they align with God's Word?

These are only a handful of questions that can begin to give us a true basis for where our hearts may be. We will end with this today and pick up tomorrow. Take some time right now to meditate on this before Jesus, and ask Him to speak His love, mercy, grace, and truth into your life. Tomorrow we will talk about how to tear down the high places and place Jesus Christ, the King of kings, back in His rightful place. I love sharing the journey of life with you!

Day 5

Verse of the day: "Now these things occurred as examples to keep us from setting our hearts on evil things as they did. Do not be idolaters, as some of them were; as it is written: 'The people sat down to eat and drink and got up to indulge in pagan revelry'" (1 Corinthians 10:6–7).

Yesterday we used Joshua's defeat and destruction of kings as a launchpad for us to consider what it is we choose to allow to rule our lives. We examined our hearts and asked ourselves some tough questions in an attempt to identify things in our lives that we may not realize we have set up as idols. In order to have a healthy, vibrant relationship with Christ, we must tear down the idols and return Jesus to His rightful position in our hearts and lives. Partial obedience in this area is not obedience at all. The Bible makes it very clear to us in scripture. Matthew 6:24 states, "No one can serve two masters. Either he will hate the one and love the other, or he will be devoted tone and despise the other. You cannot serve both God and Money." The Greek word for money in this passage is *Mamonas*. It is defined as "wealth, material possession, earthly goods, property. The comprehensive word for every kind of valuable or material good. Used only in a derogatory sense."[9] Every kind of valuable … In our list of questions yesterday, we identified things that are valuable to us. Things of value are not always material things. Our relationships are valuable us. Our children are valuable to us. Our families are valuable to us. Our time is valuable to us. Intangible things hold value for us in our lives. And *nothing is wrong* with those things meaning something to us and being valuable to us. We ought to give those things high significance in our lives. They only are sins or idols to us when they become the most important thing in our lives, rather than Jesus Christ and our relationship with Him. The children of Israel, up to this point in the Bible, have already demonstrated a challenge of the heart to stay the course and to believe God. God's Word is full of examples of the struggles of His people to keep Him on the throne of their lives, the consequences of choosing something or someone other than Him, and the delight of choosing Him and walking with Him.

How do we go about replacing the idols in our lives and tearing down the high places? How do we do this in a practical way? It begins with this verse: "Love the LORD your God with all your heart and with all your soul and with all your mind and with all your strength" (Mark 12:30). First and foremost, in tearing down idols, we must address the position of heart because idolatry is a heart issue. That verse encompasses everything required of us to place God first. He wants *all* of us. He wants our hearts, our minds, our souls, and our strength. He wants us to give Him everything we have and to serve Him and love Him with all of our beings. Yesterday, we answered some tough questions that helped us identify areas of our lives where we may not be fully living up to the command found in Mark. How a person, place, thing, or idea becomes an idol is a fairly simple process. First, it begins as a thought. Rarely do we act without the thought first entering our brains. Generally speaking, we had to have entertained a thought or an idea prior to acting on it. Our thoughts become our words and actions. Actions become patterns of living. Patterns of living then become lifestyles.

We fixate on a thought or object, and then we begin to act out of that fixation. It begins to take over our thoughts. It becomes a point of focus for us, which then replaces God's rightful place on the thrones of our lives. It becomes a high place that must be torn down so that we can grow in our relationships with Christ.

Read 2 Kings 18:1–8.

In 2 Kings 18:3–4, name the four things that Hezekiah did.

1.

2.

3.

4.

In 2 Kings 18:7, what does it specifically say Hezekiah experienced?

Hezekiah sets the perfect example of how to replace any idol in our lives with Jesus as King and Ruler of our hearts. He did what was right in the eyes of the Lord; he removed the high places. He trusted in the Lord. He did not cease to follow the Lord, and he kept the commands of the Lord. Don't you want that? Don't you want to do what is right in the eyes of the Lord? I want to delight myself in Him. His Word tells us in Psalm 37:4 that if we delight ourselves in Him, He will give us the desire of our hearts. He *becomes* the desire of our hearts. Beloved, you may be thinking you don't really know that you desire Him that way. You may be thinking this is extreme and radical. Loving Jesus *is* radical. You have to take Him at His Word when He said He came to give us life and to give it more abundantly (John 10:10). The enemy of our soul wants to destroy us and take us down. But God wants us to want Him and trust Him, and He will blow our minds with what He wants to do in our lives.

So if you don't desire Him or if this is the first you've ever considered it, ask Him to become the love of your life. Ask Him to help you desire Him. Jesus Christ is the unequivocal love of my life. He is the only One who satisfies my soul. He is the only One in whom I am completely content. I adore Him, and He delights me. He loves to delight me. He wants to delight you too. So ask Him! He will not disappoint.

Earlier we talked about how our actions begin as thoughts. We have to get our thoughts under control and submitted to the will of Christ. Second Corinthians 10:5 tells us, "We take captive every thought and make it obedient to Christ." We don't accidentally take captive our thoughts. Taking captive our thoughts is an intentional act. When we think something that does not align with the truth of scripture or that does not honor God, we must stop it in its tracks, claim the truth of God's Word in its place, and then replace it with a thought that reflects the truth of scripture. How do we know what God has to say on the matter? We must dig into His Word. We must delve into the pages of scripture, in which God reveals Himself and His will to us. It is living and active, and it transforms our hearts, thoughts, and lives. Romans 12:2 tells us "to be transformed by the renewing of our minds." It begins in our thoughts. Our actions need to follow the example of Christ in His life on this earth. Colossians 3:1–2 explains that we need to set our hearts and thoughts on things above, not earthly things. We must do what matters in eternity. Remember that God doesn't share the spotlight. God is a jealous God. We cannot serve God and also have Him share the number-one place in our lives. His holiness simply cannot abide it.

Name one recurring thought you have that you need to take captive to make it obedient to Christ.

Find a scripture that speaks truth to that thought, and write it here.

What is one action you take in order to make it obedient to Christ?

Dear sister, do you want Jesus Christ to take over your life? He is 100 percent worth it all. As we close this week, I encourage you to name an idol that has taken up residence in your life, if God has revealed it. Surrender it to Him. Ask God to show you how much better what He has for you is than any idol you could place on the throne. He is faithful, every single day.

Lord Jesus, You may have stepped on our toes today and this week, as we have spent time at Your feet, asking You to reveal to us areas of our lives where we aren't choosing to put You first. Lord, I pray that we will seek You first above all else. Jesus, help us to step out in faith and trust that whatever You want for us far exceeds anything we could ever desire for ourselves. Become the consuming passion of our lives and our hearts. Let it be reflected in our prayer lives and the outpouring of our daily living. Jesus, thank You for who You are. I adore You and want only You all the days of my life. Let us meditate and reflect on what You've taught us, and help us to not walk away unchanged. In the name above all names, I pray, amen.

WEEK FIVE

Day 1

Verse of the day: "When Joshua was old and well advanced in years, the LORD said to him, 'You are very old and there are still very large areas of land to be taken over'" (Joshua 13:1).

What we find in in Joshua 12 is the list of kings that were conquered. Thirty-one kings were named in this chapter who were defeated by the army of Israel under Joshua's leadership. That is no small amount of territory that was claimed by Israel. According to what we have previously read and studied in Joshua, the Israelites were to be thorough in their battles and take over the land of Canaan. Glance again at Joshua 13:1, our verse of the day. When God says you're very old, then you must be really old, right? This verse makes me giggle a little—because God told Joshua he was very old. My guess is Joshua already knew he was old—after all those battles, he must have been exhausted and felt his age. Goodness, after a long week, I feel my age and feel old—and I usually haven't defeated thirty-one kings in battle and assumed the territory. But perhaps I have fought my battles on a different battlefield of this life, and that's why I feel old.

As we closed out last week, we focused the last two days of study on identifying idols in our lives and devising strategies to tear them down and return God to His rightful place on the throne of our lives. Yet we battle on more than just that one front, don't we? Some weeks, it feels like we are engaged in battles from the time we first hit the snooze buttons on our alarms in the morning. Some days, it is easier to know what is attacking us. Then there are days that we feel at odds and that we can't win for the life of us because we aren't even sure what or who we are fighting.

This week, I want us to really examine our lives and identify what our personal battlefields are, as well as what our battlefield is in the spiritual realm. Once we know what our battles are, then we can arm ourselves to fight! Remember this: Jesus came to give us victory in our lives. We may not be fighting kings and conquering territory, but we are fighting our own battles every day, and there are times when that can make us feel very old. Take heart! If we are still breathing, we still have purpose in our lives.

Is there a battle that you continue to fight, over and over, in your life that makes you feel old?

Describe that battle.

Life can be very hard. Life can make us feel old in our souls and in our bodies too, can't it? It can be easy to get so caught up in the cycle of routine in our lives that we miss our purpose and lose sight of what really matters in life. Life can be a series of routines—waking up, attempting to get halfway through our never-ending to-do list, spending time with our children and families, working, maybe making dinner (if you have any energy left, or you're home early enough to fix a decent meal), going to bed, and then rising again in the morning to repeat the same thing all over again. Even in our spiritual lives, we can get caught up into a rhythm of routine and go through the motions without really letting God's Word speak into our lives and change our hearts. Satan has a heyday with that.

My favorite verse in scripture, one I would call my life verse, is Acts 20:24. This is what it says: "However, I consider my life worth nothing to me, if only I may finish the race and complete the task the Lord Jesus has given me, the task of testifying to the gospel of God's grace." What a rich and powerful verse that is full of perspective in its words. To me, this verse fuels my passions for Christ when I feel like I have nothing left in me to keep me going. It reminds me to consider my life's purpose, and that purpose is to finish this race of life, *completing* what God has called me to do—to testify to others of His gospel of grace. Hebrews 12:2–3 declares this: "Let us fix our eyes on Jesus, the author and perfector of our faith, who for the joy set before Him endured the cross, scorning its shame, and sat down at the right hand of the throne of God. Consider Him who endured such opposition from sinful men, so that you will not grow weary and lose heart."

Have you ever felt weary?

Have you ever been in a place where you feel like you have lost heart?

What did you do in those circumstances?

Perhaps you didn't know what to do. If we are not careful, life can take us down. When we are down, we lose heart and lose focus, and sometimes we forget that we can look up. It all begins with a lifting of our heads toward the heavens and a lowering of our hearts before Jesus. He is the only one who can revive a weary soul and spirit and fill us again with a passion to do His work. God's Word is ripe with verses of His sustaining power and how He breathes life into our weary souls.

Sometimes it is not just our souls that are weary. Sometimes our bodies are weary from the constant go, go, go and being pulled in multiple directions all week long. When we get to that point, we cease to do anything truly effectively. We find ourselves in desperate need of a refreshing touch of the Holy Spirit.

Read Isaiah 55:1–2.

We are beckoned to come to the Father when we are thirsty—when we are at the end our ropes and are desperate for fulfillment and refreshment. That verse speaks to me in the midst of the craziness of our culture and the materialistic nature of our society. Why do we spend our money on what doesn't satisfy? Those words were penned in biblical times. Isaiah 55:2 says. "Listen, listen to me, and eat what is good, and *your soul will delight in the richest of fare*" (emphasis added). Our souls will delight in the richest of fare when we come to Jesus and take part of what He has to offer us. Today, we can get caught up in the rat race of life, which can make us feel old and weary. On the other hand, our souls can be weary from fighting battles that feel like they are never going to end, just like Joshua (remember God told Joshua that he was old!). God doesn't want us to stay there.

Hang with me this week as we delve into our personal battlefields, inward and external, and we can devise battle strategies and arm ourselves for victory. Wherever you find yourself today, feeling old or as fresh as spring chicken, I urge you to take some time to find refuge, rest, and respite in the presence of the Father. He has our very best interests at heart, and He beckons us to come to Him for satisfaction and to recharge.

Take a few moments to write a prayer to Him today, asking for those things.

Blessings and peace, my sweet sister in Jesus.

Day 2

Verse of the day: "Fight the good fight of the faith. Take hold of the eternal life to which you were called when you made good your confession in the presence of many witnesses" (1 Timothy 6:12).

Yesterday we established that Joshua was old because God told him so—even though we fully expect that Joshua felt old due to his seven years on the battlefield at the young age of ninety-five! Joshua and the Israelites literally had to fight battles and conquer countless territories in order to claim their Promised Land. But for you and me, our battlefields look a little bit different. We aren't literally going into battle, fighting an obvious opponent to enter a tangible portion of land. Our battlefields are more subtle and require alert minds and an arsenal of spiritual weapons supplied by the Holy Spirit. As I consider my own life, I am able to comfortably ascertain that battlefields are both internal and external. Today, we will spend our time identifying what internal battlefields look like, and then tomorrow, we'll see what those external ones look like and how to combat on both fronts.

Offhand, you might not be able to quickly say, "Oh yes, this is my internal battlefield," because you may not realize there is a war raging, and you have somehow gotten sucked into it. What is the opposite of war? *Peace.* Pause a moment to consider whether or not you have peace or feel at peace in your life. Our enemy wants to rob us of peace. He is so sneaky and so sly that he watches us and waits to see where our weaknesses are in order to trip us up and knock us down. Not only does he want to knock us down, but he wants to take us down for the count!

But God—that is our key phrase for this entire study. How true is that? We can rattle off a long list of where we would be, where we should be, and so forth. *But God!* John Bradford, who was martyred for his faith by the Catholic Church, is well-known and remembered for the following statement, which is so applicable to our key phrase. He said, "There but for the grace of God go I." What does this mean? It means that only by God's grace are we able to refrain from living according to our flesh. It is God's grace that keeps us on our paths to Him, and He saves us from ourselves. Praise God! First Corinthians 15:10 says, "But by the grace of God I am what I am and his grace to me was not without effect." So while we battle—and war is all around us and within us—our God is bigger, and our God is greater. He will enable us to fight the good fight of the faith to overcome.

One of the enemy's favorite battlefields is our minds because Satan wants to take away our peace of mind. So when I say we face our internal battles, it is the battlefield of the mind. Yet each one of us faces a different enemy on the battlefield of the mind. For some, the battle lies in worrying and anxious thoughts that perpetually rob us of our peace of mind. Our minds never stop, do they? Before we can even begin to engage in warfare externally, we must win the war for our minds. Have you ever had that knot in the pit of your stomach, coupled with that sinking feeling of impending doom because your mind was racing over the same anxious thought? Our minds can run away with a worry, and we might write the most horrific outcome if we aren't careful. When we get that stirred-up, unsettled feeling—and *yes*, they do happen frequently—it is what we choose to do with those feelings and thoughts that make all the difference.

Philippians 4:6–7 tells us how to deal with those feelings: "Do not be anxious about anything, but in everything, by prayer and petition, with thanksgiving, present your requests to God. And the peace of God which transcends all understanding, will guard your hearts and minds in Christ Jesus." These verses don't promise that everything will work out exactly as we hoped or that bad things won't happen. No, they tell us how to deal with those anxious thoughts so we don't remain in a place stirred up by anxiety. We give it to God, and some days, we have to keep giving Him that same thought or worry, over and over again.

For women, one of our greatest barriers to experiencing peace of mind is insecurity or self-image. We can become so focused on that that we lose sight completely of who we are in Christ. (We'll really dig into this when we examine on day four how our internal battles affect our external lives.) Maybe we never learned who we really are in Christ and therefore cannot even begin to see ourselves as God sees us. Beloved, Jesus calls us chosen, adopted, holy, blameless, redeemed, and forgiven. Read it for yourself in Ephesians 1:3–13. This is who you are in Christ. We seem to always be striving to do better, to look better, and to improve ourselves, don't we? How much time is spent focusing on these things, rather than on who we are in Christ? Aren't we usually thinking about a diet we should be on or those pounds we need to lose? If we spent as much time obsessing over who we are in Christ and how He views us, how much more peaceful would our lives be? We would be content with ourselves because we know that our place in Him is secure, and we don't have to work to make ourselves better or good enough.

I'm not discouraging anyone from being healthy. Running is my daily dose of stress relief, after my morning coffee with Jesus, but I can become fixated on how many calories I consumed or how many I have burned. Then I think about how much I weigh, and it can be a vicious cycle, when all that should matter is how Jesus sees me. We absolutely are to take care of our bodily temples but not to the point where we are robbed of our peace of mind because we are so focused on our insecurities that we don't see Jesus anymore.

Another possible battle area that robs our minds of peace is unforgiveness or little grudges we may be holding on to in our hearts. Again, this is one internal battlefield that drastically affects our external wars. (We will delve into this one too in a few days.) Our knee-jerk reaction to the question, "Do you have any unforgiveness in your heart?" is most likely, "Absolutely not." But upon further reflection, we may discover there are hints of it lingering that we have not fully realized. In our minds, we seem to equate forgiveness with everything being okay and telling the person who wronged us that what he or she did was okay. But that's not what forgiveness is. Forgiveness is a gift we give ourselves because to do otherwise robs us of our peace of mind.

I have been forgiven so much in my life that I cannot withhold forgiveness from people who wrong me. But it's not easy. I have to ask the Holy Spirit to reveal to me where I am harboring grudges or unforgiveness in my life so He can deal with it in me. Sometimes, I have to ask God for the ability to forgive the same person for the *same wrong*, over and over again. *But God!* He enables me to forgive. Forgiveness doesn't always make the relationship return to its former state—sometimes that is not even in our best interests or what God wants—but forgiveness is for our peace of mind and because that's what God has called us to do.

Now it's your turn to do some self-reflection. There are countless other things that rob us of our peace of mind, but I highlighted some that seem to be relevant to most of us as women.

Out of the three areas mentioned above—worry, insecurity, or unforgiveness—which one do you battle with the most?

Maybe it is all three, and that's okay. Write about how that impacts your life on a daily basis.

Are you aware that this is a battle area for you?

How do you feel God wants you to respond to what you have studied today?

Write a prayer of commitment to Christ, asking for His help in fighting for your peace of mind.

God will honor your heartfelt vulnerability in this area. He is faithful, and He is trustworthy. Walk in His peace today.

Day 3

Verse of the day: "So I say, live by the Spirit, and you will not gratify the desires of the sinful nature. For the sinful nature desires what is contrary to the Spirit, and the Spirit what I contrary to the sinful nature. They are in conflict with each other, so that you do not do what you want" (Galatians 5:16–17).

All right, ladies! Are we ready to dive back into those battles we fight that make us feel old, like our Joshua we are studying? I have to tell you—my daughters and I have continued to get a kick out of this verse all week. It brings a smile to my face every time. Don't you just love how personable our God is; how intimate in our lives He wants to be? I do! Every day, He just shows me more of Himself and reinforces that He is the love of my life.

A quick recap to catch us up to today: Joshua has fought numerous battles and has spent the last seven years of his life conquering Promised Land territories, and God told him he was very old. Joshua is about to allot the land to the tribes of Israel, but we haven't gotten there yet. We are identifying the battles in our lives that make us feel old—those battles that wear us down, and make us feel like our strength is sapped. Yesterday we got into some tough stuff, identifying what our internal battles are that rob us of our peace of mind. I can't help but wonder if you meditated on that throughout the day, as I did, and asked God to reveal what other problem areas exist that attack your peace of mind. I pray God is speaking to you and revealing Himself to you in a very personal way throughout this study.

Today, it is time to reflect and determine which battles we face from the outside and the external factors that attack us. If you haven't done so already, read the verse of the day, and if you have, read it again. That verse pretty much sums up our lifelong struggle as believers on planet Earth. As Christians, praise You, Jesus, we have the indwelling of the Holy Spirit. Yet because we are human and do not yet have the glorified bodies we will receive in heaven, we still war with our sinful nature. The two are and will always be in conflict with each other. The question is, to which do we listen and submit ourselves? We are daily assaulted with attacks from the enemy, targeting our fleshly natures. These external darts fly at us everywhere we go.

Are you aware of these attacks against you as you go throughout your daily life?

From what angle are you most frequently assaulted (where do these darts occur)—for example. at home, watching TV, shopping?

Perhaps, you haven't considered these things as attacks. We live in a society and culture that conditions us to be completely desensitized to these assaults because we are so used to them. The enemy is having a field day. knowing he has us constantly under attack. Think about all the places you go during the course of a day or a week. I am all over the place because I have four children who are actively involved in sports and school life. I also work full time as a social worker and am various places through the course of the week. Due to the busyness of our lives, we are placed in many situations that allow opportunities to be attacked by the enemy. Let's begin to name these.

Regardless of our individual stage in life, most of us have a place we call home. Our homes are a favorite battleground of our enemy. He tries to wreak havoc and raise Cain in our lives at home. Several months ago, the enemy targeted one of my children. He knew how to hit me where it hurts, and boy, did he. I had gotten lax and was not being as hyper-vigilant against his schemes as I should have been, and he took advantage of that. My child was not strong enough to withstand his arrows and paid a price for his victory in her life. Satan got my attention, so I have definitely upped my game, so to speak, in being alert and proactive on the battlefront of my home. Satan wants to tear apart families and leave devastation and destruction in his wake. We, as women, cannot let him. We cannot allow ourselves to lower our guards against the enemy's schemes in our homes. It is the first place he wants to attack. He cannot have our families, but he will try. We must be aware and ready to battle for our homes.

As a result of that incident, I begun to pray fervently that God would reveal to me any areas of my home and in the lives of my children that I needed to see. God has been more than faithful in answering that prayer and revealing things to me so I could confront them and take back the territory the enemy had claimed, without my even realizing he had done it.

Can you identify a situation in which it felt like Satan was attacking your home?

If so, how did you defend your family from his attack?

What did you learn from this situation that allowed you to "up your game" so the enemy could not have the territory of your home in the future?

Let's name some other external battles we have to fight, sometimes daily. Our homes can encompass many areas we feel like we are battling. If we are mothers, sometimes it feels like we are in a never-ending battle with our children, doesn't it? Do you have days when it feels like all you do is engage in minor struggles or battles of will with your children? I know I do. And it is exhausting! Those days indeed make me feel *old*. Maybe it's not daily struggles, battles, or arguments with your children. Perhaps the battle is with a spouse. Marriage is not easy. There are times when your marriage feels like it is more battlefield than blessed union, right? That was not God's design for marriage, but it is definitely a target area for the enemy of our souls. He wants to destroy marriages. Usually, he provokes minor conflicts over insignificant things to make it more difficult to discern that he is attacking your marriage. *But God.* He is greater than the enemy of our souls and has already won the war. Satan wants us to forget that and would rather have us engage in battle against our children or spouses than zero in our focus on him and take him down. Don't let him have that territory, my sister. Jesus died on the cross for our victory in this life and for eternity. Claim His power today.

We have several more battle areas to discuss, but our homes are the hearts of our lives—our spouses, our children, our parents—whatever that looks like for you. We will stop here today to pray for our homes, children, spouses, and families. Pray against the enemy's attacks. Pray for wisdom from God to show you where you are confusing who the enemy is and engaging in battle with the wrong one.

Write your heart's plea to the Father for your home, spouse, children, and family, and ask Him to reveal to you what you need to see so you can battle against it. Ask for strength for the battle. He is faithful, and He will do it.

Day 4

Verse of the day: "Come to me, all you who are weary and burdened, and I will give you rest. Take my yoke upon you and learn from me, for I am gentle and humble in heart, and you will find rest for your souls. For my yoke is easy and my burden is light" (Matthew 11:28–30).

Are you feeling battle fatigue this week? Hang in there! God's got this, and He will enable you to not only withstand the fight but also to win the war in the name of Jesus. Thank You, Lord. Let's jump right back into the thick of things.

Yesterday we talked about the battles we face in our homes—how the enemy of our soul targets our homes, families, children, and loved ones. Those are battles we face before we ever walk out our front doors and step into the daily routines of our lives. It may not even be seven in the morning, but you're already exhausted from the battles behind the front door. Take heart, dear soul; there is indeed rest for the weary. But first, we must identify what else we fight on a daily basis. Not only do we have relationships with the individuals within our homes, but we also have relationships outside of our homes. Personally, I have felt the tensions and seen how the enemy has tried to take down my God-honoring friendships. He can so manipulate and twist things that we begin to see our friends as the enemy. This has happened in my own life, and God revealed to me that I was viewing people as the enemy and how far off base that sort of thinking was. Praise God for His spirit of wisdom and revelation.

How about this for a twist on the enemy's battle strategy for friendships—we may have friends who do not want for us the same things that Christ does, and as a result there is a broken connection with the Father. Our choice of friendships can radically affect our relationships with Christ. We are to choose our friends wisely. I'm not saying we can't be friends with unbelievers because we are to be in the world but not of it. But from whom do you chose to seek counsel? Who is in your inner circle, and are they encouraging you in your faith?

Read Psalm 1:1.

What does that say about the counsel of the wicked?

Take a moment to think about your inner circle of friends. Are they like-minded with you in the faith?

Do they encourage you to be obedient to God's Word and work in your life?

What influence do your friends have in your life?

We are beginning to see just how vital it is that we heighten our levels of awareness and alertness to the activity of the enemy in our lives. Where else in our lives do we feel is always a battle? For some, it is finances. We feel like we can never get ahead, or maybe we feel this need to keep up with the Joneses, so we consistently keep our family finances strained. This can cause personal stress and tension as well as with our spouses or children. God will provide for us, but He also expects us to be good stewards of the things He has entrusted to us. Don't let the enemy take ground in your finances. Related to finances is the professional world. Work-related stress and tensions can become battlefields. We can feel like this area is always a battle. Think about the impact of work stress on your personal life. Whew! Life can be exhausting, can't it?

We can't discuss the external battles we face without addressing the one that assaults us everywhere we go. Let's talk about the barrage of fiery arrows that are shot at us from our current culture and society. Our culture bombards us with messages that are in complete opposition to what God has to say in the Bible. This is such an effective means of warfare for the enemy. The messages we receive from our culture sound like this:

Do what feels right to you.

There are no absolutes.

Your truth is the only truth that matters.

It's all about you! Put yourself first!

There are no wrongs.

Sleep with whomever you love at the moment.

Marriage is whatever you want it to be.

Beauty is on the outside.

Money can buy happiness—just try it!

This latest diet is what will make you beautiful.

This isn't even the tip of the iceberg of what our culture is telling us—and our families. We cannot let our culture claim our territory. The battle is exhausting, and it can feel overwhelming because we cannot escape living in our world, this side of heaven. So we must battle it. That is our only option. We can battle it by what we allow ourselves to watch on TV, the types of music we listen to, the books and magazines we read, and the stores where we shop. Victory is not accidental; it is deliberate. We must be intentional in our battles so that we do not slip up. It is exhausting, and we can feel worn down. That is when we are at our weakest.

Movies and TV shows us encourage us to just step out in that illicit affair because that's what makes it exciting. *But God.* He says marriage is beautiful, and that is where it is most exciting. I urge you, dear sister, when confronted on this battlefront, to look to scripture, and see what God has to offer. I promise you it is more enticing and more satisfying than anything you will choose, apart from God. We must remind ourselves what is found in 1 Peter 2:9–12.

> But you are a chosen people, a royal priesthood, a holy nation, a people belonging to God, that you may declare the praises of him who called you *out of darkness* into his wonderful light. Once you were not a people, but now you are the *people of God*; once you had not received mercy, but now you have received mercy. Dear friends, I urge you, *as aliens and strangers in the world, to abstain from sinful desires which war against your soul.* Live such good lives among the pagans, that, though they accuse you of doing wrong, they may see your good deeds and glorify God on the day he visits us. (Emphasis added.)

Where do you feel most vulnerable to the enemy, regarding cultural impact and influence?

How are you able to stand firm?

What are the sinful desires that wage war against your soul?

Be encouraged, my sister! God has given us everything we need to stand firm, to not be war-weary, and to endure until the end. Tomorrow we will discuss our battle strategies and how to be victorious. This week has taken a bit of a detour from the book of Joshua, but the questions and the content stemmed from Joshua's several years of battle prior to claiming the Promised Land territory. It is imperative that we realize this daily life of battling is not the end result. It would be so easy to get caught up in the here-and-now that we lose sight and lose focus of the eternal significance of our earthly lives. But we must persevere!

Read again the verse of the day. Jesus beckons us to come to Him because we are the weary and the heavy-laden. More days than not, that is what I feel like. I feel like Joshua, when God told him he was old. Seven straight years of battle, but my guess is that in the end, Joshua would have said it was totally worth it. We face so many more types of battles daily. We cannot begin to name them all. What we can do is look to the One who offers us victory, peace, and rest in Him. Don't let Satan distract you with the daily battles of life. Even in the midst of those, we can choose to honor God with our attitudes, responses, actions, and words.

We live in a world that wants something more, but unbelievers don't know what that "more" is. So they are watching believers, waiting to see if it works for us and to see if is real and if it lasts. Point others to Jesus by how you choose to face the battle. Let it be said of us as Paul states it: "Follow my example, as I follow the example of Christ" (1 Corinthians 11:1).

Day 5

Verse of the day: "Put on the full armor of God so that you can take your stand against the devil's schemes" (Ephesians 6:11).

Be encouraged! God does not leave us to battle on our own. It is not a solo fight for us. He does not leave us to our own devices and wish us well. No, God has already won the war, but He also has left us with His Spirit inside of us, as we engage in the battles of everyday life.

First Peter 5:8–9 says, "Be self-controlled and alert. Your enemy the devil prowls around like a roaring lion looking for someone to devour. Resist him, standing firm in the faith, because you know that your brothers throughout the world are undergoing the same kind of sufferings."

Our first line of defense against the devil in the battle is this. Know who your true enemy is. While we battle daily, we need to remember that all we face are schemes of the enemy—he is disguising himself behind all the various fronts we face, but he is the mastermind behind them all. Never lose sight of who the true enemy is. When we feel exhausted from the battles, it is because our enemy has worn us down. Never forget who is trying to bring us down. We follow the words in 1 Peter 5—be self-controlled and be alert. Other versions of the Bible use the word "sober," rather than self-controlled. Both render the same implication that we must have our spiritual priorities in alignment with God's Word, and we must be alert. We must not be careless or reckless but be aware of the enemy and his proximity as he prowls around us, looking for ways to destroy us. Satan is the master manipulator, and he will disguise his lies as half-truths and make them so appealing to us because he knows our weakness—this is why we must have our spiritual priorities in the right place.

Read Ephesians 6:10–18.

This is such a familiar passage, but I pray that the importance and significance of the words in these verses are not lost on you. This is how we gear up for battle.

Ephesians 6:10 tells us to be strong in the Lord and His mighty power. This power is applicable to *all* the areas in which we are tempted, we battle, and we encounter.

We have one day to hit the highlights of this passage—entire Bible studies have been completed on these verses. Let's pray God will fill our cups with whatever we need to drink from individually to empower us in our battle.

Why are we to put on the full armor of God? (Ephesians 6:11).

Who are we *not* battling?

Who are we battling? (Name all four.)

Again we are reminded that our enemy is not flesh and blood—so we better be on guard to not make enemies of the individuals God has placed in our lives. The true enemy is the enemy of our souls. The enemy is not our spouses, our children, our parents, our in-laws, our coworkers, or our bosses. Satan will masquerade as long as he can, in order to convince us differently. How do we then combat against the work of the enemy within and among our relationships? One way to do so is found in Colossians 3:12–14.

"Therefore, as God's chosen people, holy and dearly loved, clothe yourselves with compassion, kindness, humility, gentleness, and patience. Bear with each other and forgive whatever grievances you may have against one another. Forgive as the Lord forgave you. And over all these virtues, put on love, which binds them all together in perfect unity."

Imagine what your relationships would look like if you clothed yourself daily in these attributes. Would it not impact your entire world? Because we are God's dearly loved, chosen daughters, we should begin each day by getting dressed. What should we wear? The answer to that question has never been so clear-cut. (As a woman, don't you just hate trying to decide what to wear every day?) We now have the answer.

Get dressed in some compassion, some kindness, a whole lot of humility, gentleness, patience, forgiveness, and love. We cannot clothe ourselves in these without the binding quality of love. We have the love of Jesus flowing through us, so we are compelled love others. It is contrary to who we are in Christ. What does love look like?

Read 1 Corinthians 13:4–8.

What does love look like when we wear it every day?

Before we even begin to arm ourselves for battle, let's first get dressed in the clothes we should wear as believers. All right, now back to our armor found in Ephesians 6. The ultimate goal of arming ourselves is found in Ephesians 6:13. Paul says, "Therefore put on the full armor of God, so that when the day of evil comes, you may be able to stand your ground, and after you have done everything, to stand." The goal here is that we withstand the assaults of the enemy without faltering or wavering. Count the number of times you see the word "stand" in this passage. Four times, with three in just verses 13 and 14. When something is repeated in scripture multiple times, we should take note of the message God is giving to us. He has equipped us with all we need to *stand firm*. When we stand firm, we are not easily pushed over. Think about that physical image for a minute. If someone tells you to stand firm, you will plant your feet and brace your legs so that you will not easily budge. That's what God wants us to do spiritually. How do we go about doing this? We put on armor daily—that's how!

What gets buckled around our waists?

Picture a soldier from those days. They wore tunics, and prior to fighting, they put on a belt—a girdle, of sorts—in order to tighten up all the cloth that hung loosely. Otherwise, they were at risk in battle. Truth will bind up the things that hinder us. You have to know the truth to use it in battle.

What is the next piece of armor?

The breastplate of righteousness guards our hearts, just like the breastplate protects the vital organs of a soldier in combat. As believers, we have the righteousness of Christ, and to live in opposition to His holiness leaves us at risk of attack from the enemy. Our hearts must be guarded, above all else, with the righteousness of Christ.

Name the next piece of armor.

The shoes of the Roman soldier had nails on the bottom to help them keep their feet planted and to stand firmly. The gospel of peace is the message of our salvation that provides us peace with God.

The shield of faith comes next—this shield protects the whole body in battle. We can use our faith as a defensive weapon against the enemy. We have faith that God will give us victory. We have faith that God will not leave us unprotected from the temptations the enemy hurls at us in an effort to make us fall. We have faith that God is more than able to do more than we can imagine. We can use our shields of faith to believe God, take Him at His word, and not be manipulated by the lies of the enemy.

Put on the helmet of salvation.

What is the purpose of a helmet?

To protect the head, right? Our thoughts need to be protected from the lies of the enemy. He will try to trip us up. He will try to convince us that we are not truly saved. He will try to mix us up in our feelings. The helmet of salvation protects our thoughts and minds from the enemy. The only offensive weapon we are told to put on here is the sword of the Spirit.

What is our sword?

Sister, we have to know what the Word says in order to use it in battle. If that's not a motivator to dig in and learn God's truth, then I don't know what is.

Finally, we are told to pray. Our greatest offense and defense against the enemy is to pray. *Pray, pray, pray!* When we focus our minds in prayer and cultivate a lifestyle of prayer, we have guarded ourselves against the enemy in ways we don't even see. Never let your prayer life go stagnant or lukewarm. That leaves you at greatest risk and vulnerability.

Describe your prayer life.

Upon reflection, do you feel it has been an effective weapon against the enemy in your life? Why or why not?

We began this week by reading God's words to Joshua in Joshua 13:1. Read that again, right now. As we outlined and identified the various battles we face, I felt the weariness of always being in battle. After today, though, I feel recharged, refreshed, and ready to fight. I know what clothes to wear underneath all of that armor that will pave the way to honoring Christ in my relationships. I am encouraged to gear up for battle because I know who has already won the war for me on the cross of Calvary! Hallelujah, and thank You, Jesus! Be encouraged with me today.

Father, as we close another week of study, I am in awe of Your goodness and humbled by Your faithfulness. You have loved me at my very worst. You have redeemed this life from the pit in order to use it for Your honor and glory. I pray that we will daily clothe ourselves as Your holy and dearly loved children. I pray that You pour Your

Holy Spirit afresh upon us, and bless the time spent getting to know what You have to say to us in Your Word. I love You, Lord Jesus. You are the truest desire of my heart and the satisfaction of my soul. In Your so very beautiful and sweet name of Jesus, amen.

WEEK SIX

Day 1

Verse of the day: "Then the land has rest from war" (Joshua 14:15b).

At long last, the Israelites had conquered the land that had been promised to them and divisions and allotments were made for each tribe. The next several chapters, Joshua 13–19, outline exactly which territories each tribe received. We will not take these chapter by chapter because if you're like me, your eyes tend to stop understanding what you're reading due to all the names and locations that you simply couldn't put on a map, ancient or otherwise. The boundary lines for each tribe of Israel are important but not pertinent to our study. We can, however, make some points and draw some parallels. Please read through these chapters, if you want. At the very least, skim through those next several chapters to familiarize yourself with the tribes of Israel. Some of the significance in these verses is not felt until the story of Joshua has come to a close. For our intent and purpose, those verses are the ones that state that some of the territories were not completely wiped out. The impact of not doing so creates future issues within the nation of Israel. (See Joshua 16:10; 17:12–18.)

Isn't that just a little bit like us? God has provided victory in battle for the Israelites to drive out the enemy and take over the land He had promised to them, but they still withheld complete obedience to Him—after everything! Wandering in the wilderness for forty years taught them a lot, but apparently there were still lessons to be learned. But we do that. When we look at all that Christ did for us on the cross of Calvary—where our justification was given and bestowed upon us with the fullest measure of grace, in spite of our total lack of deserving this gift—how could we possibly want to withhold any part of ourselves from Him? When we consider His ongoing process of sanctification in our lives, how can we not pour our lives out before Him in total surrender? Yet we don't always do that. Sometimes we deceive ourselves into thinking that in the grand scheme of things, holding on to this or that will not affect us or hurt anyone else. The more we tell ourselves this, the more convinced we become that it is true.

Can you think of an example of this form of self-deception and its potential consequences?

We would be wise to be vigilant and on high alert in order to spare ourselves—and possibly those we love—from the consequences of partial obedience. Partial obedience is essentially disobedience. In our world, we don't like to use words like obedience or disobedience. As a parent, I am careful not to use those words when referring to any adult other than myself or God in the lives of my children. Our tendency is to bristle when hearing the word "obey." Isn't that just like our sin nature?

"Submit" is another one of those words that raises defiance in our flesh. *But God.* His way is truly not our way. His ways are for our benefit, and that includes obedience, submission, and surrender—three battles we daily have to fight. Paul discusses this ongoing battle in Romans 7. Turn there and read verses 15–25.

Now, that's a lot to wrap your mind around, isn't it?! Yet when I read those verses, I can totally relate. When I read it, I feel like Paul got inside of my mind and wrote on paper exactly the battle I feel. Until we reach heaven, we will not achieve glorification, which is the freedom from this body of flesh and bones. Justification occurred for us on Calvary. It was the one-time price Christ paid for the penalty of our sins. Sanctification is the ongoing process of our becoming more like Christ—it is the state that we, as Christians, currently are. We are in the process of allowing Christ to make us more like Him. But as it clearly points out in Romans 7, the war between our sin nature and the Spirit living in us rages on. What we want to do, we don't do, and what we don't want to do, we do! As Paul describes the struggle, he finally just says, "What a wretched man I am!" (Romans 7:24).

Can you relate to that struggle?

What struggle in your life does your mind automatically think of when you read these verses?

Praise God for His sanctifying work in our lives. He doesn't leave us in our wretched state. On our own, without the blood of Christ covering us, we are hopeless, and we do not stand a chance in our flesh. *But God!* He loves us so much that He didn't want to leave us in that state. Even after He saved us, He didn't leave us alone and on our own to fight against our flesh. Praise You, Lord, for that grace. Our verse for the day in Joshua tells us simply that the land was at rest from the war. Breathe a huge sigh of relief! Doesn't that just sound refreshing—to be at rest from the war? But guess what? We too, in spite of the flesh versus the spirit, can have rest, even in the midst of it all. Are you asking how? We just read about the constant struggle between what we want to do and don't want to do, yet we do it anyway. What is the answer to rest from war in our lives? Surrender! Surrendering is waving the white flag—an agreement to cease fighting. Surrendering is submitting. We surrender ourselves to Christ—we lay aside all that is *us* that is in us, and we give to Christ to complete the work He so desires within us and through us.

What does surrender look like in the life of a believer? I am so glad you asked! So many times, as Christians, we "know" what we are supposed to do, but we don't really *know* what that actually looks like when lived out. We will see what scripture says about surrendering ourselves and experiencing rest in our lands from war.

Read Romans 12:1.

What are we instructed to do here with our bodies?

How would you describe a living sacrifice?

Read Galatians 2:20, and write it here:

Who was crucified with Christ?

Who now lives in us?

How do we live, then?

Read Philippians 2:5–8.

What did Christ make Himself as?

What two things did He do, according to Philippians 2:8?

Now look back at Philippians 2:5, and write how verses 6 through 8 should affect us.

Do you see the connections here, my friend? We are to completely die to ourselves—we have been crucified with Christ. He was raised back to life, but we can remain dead to sin and live for Christ. We make a choice to daily surrender ourselves to Jesus and choose to live how He wants us to live. We should adopt the same attitude as Christ, who so completely humbled Himself that He was obedient to die on that same cross. May we humble ourselves daily to walk in obedience and total surrender to Him. This death to ourselves ultimately offers us the most satisfying, most fulfilling life we can live. Surrender provides us with much-needed rest.

Matthew 16:24–25 says this: "Then Jesus said to His disciples, 'If anyone would come after me, he must deny himself and take up his cross and follow me. For whoever wants to save his life will lose it, but whoever loses his life for me will find it.'" Denying ourselves. Dying to ourselves. Losing our lives. All of these concepts are completely backwards to the way our culture and society and *our sin nature* operate. *But God.* He desires so much more for us than we can even begin to wrap our minds around. His way offers us peace, rest, and freedom.

What do you need to surrender today? I encourage you to take Jesus at His Word. Tell Him today what you need to surrender, ask Him for the courage to do so, and trust Him to be worth it. Close today by writing that prayer to Him.

Day 2

Verse of the day: "So the Israelites divided the land, just as the LORD had commanded Moses" (Joshua 14:5).

Are you ready to enter your Promised Land? Yesterday we finished our day with writing a prayer of surrender to Christ—surrendering ourselves in order to move forward in the rest and freedom He has to offer us.

Where are you currently in your stage of life?

How would you describe your attitude toward your current state in life? For example, are you content, restless, or anxious, or do you feel like there should be more? Be honest and thoughtful in your answer.

The Promised Land seems, at times, elusive to us, as if we might never reach it. The Israelites, under the leadership of Moses, did not enter their Promised Land. To me, that is the most saddening—to live life on planet Earth and reach the end of your time here, never having arrived in your Promised Land, having missed the opportunity to do so. What happened? What prevented them from entering the land God had promised them? Hebrews 3:19 gives us the simple answer. "So we see that they were not able to enter, because of their unbelief." Read Deuteronomy 1:19–45. This is the full account of why they spent forty years wandering in the wilderness. The unbelief of the nation of Israel cost them the fulfillment of God's promises to them during their lifetimes. Wouldn't that be devastating? They got in their own way. They messed it up for themselves. There's a reason why this is all documented on the pages of scripture for us—so we can learn from their mistakes and never forget the faithfulness of God. Oh, that we would not make the same mistakes in our lives. We have a choice to make—live within the safe confinement of what we know, or step out in faith and obedience to all God has for us.

I pray that you already are doing this—that you know and believe that all God has for you is beyond your mind and imagination, and you are living it out. Oh, how I pray that is where you are today. The safest place you will ever find yourself is in the center of God's will. Or maybe you are feeling the promptings of the Holy Spirit. and you can sense that God is laying on your heart to do something specific, and you are hesitating, right on the edge of making that step. I urge you to take it. One foot in front of the other, and God will blow your mind!

For the nation of Israel, the Promised Land was actual land, territories divided among the tribes of Jacob. It was a land flowing with milk and honey. For us, that is symbolic of fullness and sweetness. Oh, how precious and sweet is living life with Jesus. Intimacy with Jesus. Satisfaction in a relationship with Him. Contentment with life because of Christ. That is our Promised Land, sweet sister. To be close to Christ this side of heaven and know He is our very best friend.

He is your refuge, your rescuer. He is the delight of your heart. He is the one who knows all there is to know about you and still loves you and *wants* to hang out with you every single day. He is the one who will *never* leave you alone. He is your courage. He is hope. He is more than you could ever need or want. He is the satisfaction of your soul. He makes this life worth it for you. Having that kind of relationship with Him makes you laugh out loud in happiness and delight—fullness and sweetness. "Taste and see that the Lord is good" (Psalm 34:8). Your Promised Land can be experienced wherever you are—when you take that step in faith and believe that God is all that He says He is and that He fulfills all the promises He has bestowed on you.

Our current situations in life may not make it feel very much like a Promised Land, but our attitudes toward our circumstances can certainly provide us the opportunity to view it as such. God wants to use us where He has placed us. Read Acts 17:26, and be in awe! He determined the times set for us and the exact places where we live.

How do you feel when you read that verse?

God chose to place us on this earth when He did because He has plans for our lives. He has plans for an abundant life for us. He does not desire that we go through life, riding the tide of mediocrity and missing His purpose for us. God has a specific plan and specific purpose for every single one of us. He wants us to lean on Him, to trust Him, and to believe in Him as we journey through this life, so that we can fulfill what He has placed us here to do. God created each one of us uniquely. He created us with dreams, interests, talents, gifts, and passions. He didn't give us these to not ever use them. He didn't allow our hearts to build dreams, only to ask us daily to stuff them down. He wants us to use those specific gifts, talents, interests, and even dreams to accomplish His purposes and to bring honor and glory to His name. Doesn't that amaze you?

God wants us to enjoy spending our lives serving Him. When we combine our unique interests, talents, desires, and dreams with God's purpose for our lives, we can say we have arrived at the Promised Land! Living life sold out for Christ *is* the abundant life. I love Jesus so much. He is everything I want. He is the love of my life. I want so badly for every other woman to love Him like this. He determines my steps. He defines who I am. He is the reason I get out of bed in the morning. He is my delight and my heart's true one desire. I adore Him. I am in awe of Him. He is very much alive and active, and I cannot get enough of Him. He is more than enough for me. He is, truly, everything to me. I cannot imagine ever living life apart from Him again.

I don't want anyone to miss out. I want everyone to want Him like this. God uses that desire for His glory. My past is messy. I don't have a neat, clean story. But God is the one who has woven my life into this beautiful tapestry of grace, healing, forgiveness, and love. There are dreams in my heart that remain, and I entrust them to the Father and ask Him to please make them come to pass, if He can use them. But I trust that if it's not His will, then that's okay because I want what He wants for me even more. Intimacy with Jesus Christ *is* the Promised Land.

At the beginning of the day, I asked about your current situation in life. After reading today's lesson, does it change your attitude toward your situation?

If so, how?

How would you describe your personal Promised Land, unique to you?

Let's not be like the Israelites, who let their unbelief derail their entire life course, and miss all that God wants for us. First Corinthians 2:9 tells us this: "However, as it is written: 'No eye has seen, no ear has heard, no mind has conceived what God has prepared for those who love Him.'"

Day 3

Verse of the day: "So on that day Moses swore to me, 'The land on which your feet have walked will be your inheritance and that of your children forever, because you have followed the LORD my God wholeheartedly'" (Joshua 14:9).

In the beginning of the study, we talked about Joshua's being one of the two spies who believed that God would enable Israel to claim the land God had promised them. We asked questions about what made him different from all the others. The other individual, his fellow spy who scoped out the land with him, was Caleb. Caleb was the only other one who was able to enter the Promised Land. In our verse of the day, Moses was speaking to Caleb, not Joshua. Caleb was up there in age with Joshua, about eighty-five years old, but he was now receiving his inheritance at long last. God honors our love and obedience to Him. First Samuel 15:22 provides us insight into what God wants from us. "Does the LORD delight in burnt offerings and sacrifices as much as in obeying the voice of the LORD? *To obey is better than sacrifice*, and to heed is better than the fat of rams" (emphasis added).

Obedience is better than sacrifice. The posture of the heart is more important than the outward actions. Read that again, and let it absorb. At the time when the Old Testament was written, Jesus clearly had not come to earth. There were strict instructions on how, when, and where to sacrifice and for what purposes. We are not under the Law but under grace, so we aren't required to make burnt offerings and sacrifices on altars. Christ was our once-for-all sacrifice. So the Old Testament Jews could offer sacrifices, but no one could see the condition of their hearts. They could carry out these sacrifices without ever being obedient to God in their daily lives. That's why we read what we read in 1 Samuel about obedience. God desires our obedience, not just sacrifices. Caleb was recognized by Moses as one who wholeheartedly followed the instructions of God. He was obedient. As a result, he received his inheritance.

So many life applications can be made from both Caleb's and Joshua's examples to us in scripture and from the verse in 1 Samuel. We may not be under the Law, as in Old Testament days, but what God desires from us remains the same. Our Father also desires our obedience, rather than sacrifice. It is a matter of the heart—the attitude behind the action—that God is really looking at. For example, we know God tells us to put on kindness and to be kind to one another. However, if we are kind to someone by making him or her a meal, but we complain to everyone in our home about it, while plastering a smile on our faces as we deliver the goods, what is our heart attitude behind the outward expression of kindness?

Give your own example of obedience being better than sacrifice.

As a result of Caleb's obedience, he received his inheritance. We too, as believers, have a spiritual inheritance. First and foremost, our spiritual inheritance is Jesus Christ Himself. Hallelujah! We have eternity with Christ. We have *right now* with Christ! We will never be taken out of His hand. We may choose to walk away from Him and turn our backs on Him, but if we are truly His, no one can pluck us from His hand (John 10:28–29). When Christ returns, He is coming back for us! We get to be the friends of God if we obey His commands (John 15:14).

Read 1 Peter 1:3–9.

What kind of hope do we have?

What two things has Christ given us through His resurrection?

Describe the inheritance.

What is the goal of our faith? (1 Peter 1:9).

Sister, our inheritance is kept by God's power. Regardless of our earthly circumstances, our inheritance through Jesus Christ is secure. We are secure in Christ. We are daily saved from the power of sin in our lives while we also wait for the ultimate goal of our faith, which is eternity in heaven with Christ. We can withstand any and every thing life throws at us because of our inheritance in Christ. We can look past the immediacy of the circumstances and keep our eyes fixed on the cross because we have a hope and an inheritance that will not fade or spoil or perish. Praise God! These are secure in Jesus Christ! My question to you, then, is this: do you live like your inheritance is Jesus Christ? Do you live in such a way that reflects that this earth is not your home? Do you live in such a way that reflects you can withstand and endure the trials you face because of your inheritance?

We do not face each day like unbelievers. We can rise in the mornings, knowing that our hope is in Christ, that we are daily given the power over sin through Christ, and we trust that God can use whatever we encounter during the day for our own good. He can also use us in whatever position we find ourselves throughout the day. It doesn't matter where we work, where we live, or what we are doing—we can glorify Christ and behave in such a way that demonstrates to the world that our faith and our hope is in Jesus. We can work in the secular world and still act in ways that set us apart and spread the light of Christ. Every day, we are on the mission field. Our inheritance is Christ Jesus. It is incorruptible. And there is more than enough for everyone to partake! We must not keep it to ourselves! We are not called to hide it.

Reflect on that for a minute, and respond to the question: do you live like your inheritance is Jesus Christ?

Now read Ephesians 1:3–17.

I don't know if your Bible has headers, but if so, go back to see what it says before the start of verse 3. My Bible refers to this passage as "Spiritual Blessings in Christ." What are those blessings? To sum it up, we were chosen before the foundation of the world to be holy and blameless. We are predestined and adopted as God's children—*because* it was His will, and it pleased Him. Isn't that amazing? It pleased God to adopt us as His children. He chose us to be His children. If you ever doubt you are loved, *don't* doubt it! God loves you so very much.

We are redeemed and forgiven. He lavished His grace on us with wisdom and understanding. God has a plan that includes choosing us in order to fulfill His will. We are included in Christ—wow! We were marked with the Holy Spirit who was promised, guaranteeing our inheritance. That is eternity with Christ. The daily inheritance of being His child—power over sin—and the eternal inheritance, which is eternity with Him. God desires relationships with us. Look at all the things He has given to us through His Son, Jesus, and His work on the cross. That is how much God desires us to live life with Him every single day. He wants us to walk with Him. He wants to have an intimate relationship with us. He made it possible for us to do so. He doesn't want to be a distant observer of our everyday lives and only occasionally be invited in for a visit. No, no, *no*! He wants to be present and actively involved because we desire to place Him in that role. Our inheritance in Christ is by far, the most desired Promised Land we could ever ask for. Doesn't that excite you?

What role do you allow Christ to have in your life? Is He living it out with you? Or do you place Him at a distance from your actual life?

Respond to what Christ has revealed to you today. Write either a prayer of commitment to making Him an active part of your life or a prayer of praise to Him for all He has blessed you with and for being so intimately involved in the day-to-day living.

Day 4

Verse of the day: "So be very careful to love the LORD your God" (Joshua 23:11).

We are drawing close to the end of studying the book of Joshua. For week 7, we will do something a bit different to retain the important things God has shown us throughout the study. But hang in there as we dig in for the next two days to see what final lessons we can learn from this book. Begin today by reading Joshua 23.

Where we begin today in Joshua, many years have passed since they settled into their allotted territories. Again, we see that Joshua was acknowledged as being very old (even older than the last time we were told he was old), and he has called together the leaders of Israel to deliver one of his final two speeches. Beginning in verse 3 and continuing to verse 5, he reminds them of how God fought for them and used Joshua to drive out their enemies from the land. Verses 6–13 contain an admonition for strength and a firm warning against adapting to the nations around them. Verses 14–16 are a reminder of God's faithfulness to keep His promises and the significance of keeping covenant with the Lord. In each of these sections, we can apply the concepts to our daily lives.

1. Remember what God has done for us. Though many years have passed since the Israelites were at war, Joshua reminded them not to forget that it was God who drove the enemies out of the Promised Land. In addition, that same land was given to them as their inheritance. The emphasis in this passage is on remembering what God did. Why did they have to be reminded that God had done these things for them? That question resonates within me. Look at all God had done. Surely they had not forgotten. How could they possibly, right? Yet ... don't we do that? In the immediacy of circumstances in which we needed the Lord Jesus to show up for us and come through, and He does, we know that there was no other way for us to have survived the situation in one piece except through the power of the Holy Spirit. Our faith grows exponentially during that time of life, and we think there is no way we could lose the feeling or forget God's faithfulness to us. Then, time goes by. Years pass. The memory of the situation fades away. If we aren't careful, we forget just how faithful God was to us during that time. We may even begin to remember it a little differently than how it happened. A little bit of pride may creep in, and we may begin to give ourselves more credit than we ought for how we handled that situation, circumstance, or season. Or we simply begin to drift right back into our old patterns of thinking and behaving as time goes on. There is a reason that Joshua began his speech with a reminder of God's faithfulness. They needed to remember that it was only through God's faithfulness that they were where they were at that time. Even though years had passed, God's faithfulness remained the same, and it was through nothing of their own doing that got them there.

We too need to remind ourselves to remember all God has done for us. It may not even pertain to a particular season when God demonstrated His faithfulness to us in unforgettable ways. It could merely be living with the daily awareness of God's grace, *just to make it through the day.* Have you ever stopped to imagine what your day would look like if you didn't have the power of the Holy Spirit living in you? Think about it! We mess it up even then. Just imagine if we were left to our own devices without the Spirit working in us and through our speech, behaviors, and relationships. Daily, we need to remember God's faithfulness to us, in the little things as well as the huge things in life. How do we do that? It only happens through being intentional about remembering. For each one of us, that may look different.

By remembering God's faithfulness in our lives, we also remain humble. Humility is a key component of the Christian walk. Scripture tells us that if we don't humble ourselves, then God will do it for us. I don't know about you, but I would prefer to take on the posture of humility rather than being broken down in order to remain humble. Remember God's faithfulness, sister.

What would a day look like if you were left to your own devices without the Holy Spirit working in you?

Describe a specific time when God showed up in a way that only could have been Him.

Did it impact your walk with Him?

How have you been able to remember that, in order to not forget His faithfulness as time goes on?

What are some ways that would work for you personally to remember all God's faithfulness in even the smaller, daily areas of living?

2. Refuse to become like the world around us. What a high calling in the world in which we now live. Back in the days of Joshua, he admonished them to obey all that was written in the Law of Moses—not to look away from it and get caught up into the ways of the nations around them. He warned them against serving their gods and stressed the importance of holding fast to the Lord. He went on to tell them to be very careful to love the Lord, as we read in our verse of the day.

You aren't careful accidentally. It is intentional. It requires discipline, steadfastness, and a focused heart and mind. So many things creep into our lives, don't they? We are constantly being pushed, tugged, pulled, made to feel guilty, shamed, and even manipulated into becoming like the world around us. But we are not to conform. Whether you are serving yourself and the things of the world or serving Christ, it does not just happen. Earlier in the study we talked about the impact of our minds and our thoughts on our behaviors. The same concept applies in this scenario. Don't you want to be intentional in loving Jesus? Look at the words Joshua uses to describe the influence of the other nations on Israel: snares, traps, whips on their backs, thorns in their eyes, and, ultimately, perishing in the land.

What things or temptations in your life have the potential to become snares, whips, traps, and thorns if you are not carefully loving Jesus and eradicating them?

Read Ephesians 5:1–7.

List the six things that should not be present in the lives of the believer.

Going on further in that chapter, Paul tells them to have nothing to do with the fruitless deeds of darkness. Fruitless deeds of darkness surround us. The enemy attempts to oppress with the things in his realm. This world is his playground, and he delights in the deeds of darkness. If we are not intentional in loving Jesus, we will succumb. We are to put on the new self that is created to be like God in true righteousness and holiness (Ephesians 4:24). That is our calling. We are to be in the world, not of the world. We are to be lights in this dark world. Where is the line? Jesus ate with sinners and hung out with them. He even said He came to save the sinner, not the righteous. We are commissioned to go out into the world and win souls for Christ. We can't shine light in an already lit room, right? But again, where is the line?

We can take advantage of the situation, push the limits on the line, and use it as an excuse to indulge in the desires of the flesh. Think about your realms of influence. Shine light there. Don't be afraid to take a stand for Christ and to be different. Love the people in the world like Christ does. Then there is no question of where the line is. We don't have to conform to share love and to show love.

Where can you shine the light and love of Christ in your world even today?

I challenge you to try it! To take one small step out of your comfort zone, and do it.

3. Remain faithful to the covenant as God remains faithful to us. Look at Joshua 23:14–16. Joshua tells them again that God has been faithful to His covenant with them and will uphold His covenant with them for good, if they are obedient—or for their not-so-good, if they are disobedient. God is faithful to us. He remains true to who He is, no matter the number of days and years that pass. He is a just God. Remember that holy fear and reverence we learned about? This is an example of the same type of thing. As believers, we need to remain faithful to God through it all. Galatians 5:1 tells us this: "It is for freedom that Christ has set us free. Stand firm, then, and do not let yourselves be burdened again by a yoke of slavery." We get to be free because of Christ's redemptive work on the cross—don't let that be in vain. Paul urges us to stand firm. We can remain faithful because of Christ. He has set us free. We don't have to return to our former state as slaves. Hallelujah! We no longer live to satisfy the desires of our flesh ... no, praise God, He has changed our desires and we can stand firm in a world that is threatening to close in around us. Be of good cheer, Christ tells us, because He has overcome the world.

Day 5

Verse of the day: "After these things, Joshua son of Nun, the servant of the LORD, died at the age of a hundred and ten. And they buried him in the land of his inheritance at Timnath Serah in the hill country of Ephraim, north of Mount Gaash" (Joshua 24:29–30).

Begin today by reading Joshua 24.

Joshua gathered all of Israel together to deliver his final speech. Can you just imagine the scene? Years have passed since they settled into their new homes. Their beloved and great leader, now even older than old, has gathered them together to speak a final time to the tribes of Israel. His speech begins with the retelling of all that God has done for the nation of Israel, beginning with Abraham. Just imagine sitting there, listening to him tell the story of your ancestors and hearing again of God's unfailing faithfulness to them, knowing this also is your story. Joshua instructs them again to fear the Lord and serve Him with faithfulness (Joshua 24:14–15), but he also tells them it is their choice who they will serve. He gives them their options. Then he declares that he and his household will serve the Lord. After hearing the account of God's faithfulness to Israel through all of it, how could they not declare that they were going to serve the one true God?

The people responded to Joshua's words and answered they were going to serve the Lord. Joshua warned them of the outcome of their turning aside from God and serving other gods—it would be disaster! The people again replied they wanted to serve God. Joshua told them to get rid of the foreign gods they had among them. The thought occurred to me as I read this chapter that the reason Joshua mentioned their choices of whom to serve was because some of them were not choosing to serve the Lord.

Again, time had passed. They had settled into their new lives and new routines, and some of them even adapted the cultures around them. (May that not ever be said of us, girls. Stand firm. Stay strong until the end. It will be worth it. God promises!) One final time, Joshua made a covenant before the people of Israel. He set up a stone near the holy place as a witness to their covenant to serve the Lord. I love how it is phrased in the New International Version of the Bible: "Then Joshua sent the people away, each to his own inheritance" (Joshua 24:28). Again, there was the reminder that God was faithful to His promises, and they received the land of promise—their inheritance! Joshua lived to be 110 years old and died having received the land of his inheritance. He was faithful to the Lord, serving Him and trusting Him.

Joshua died knowing he had completed what God intended for him to do. The greatest tragedy in life is to not finish strong in the faith and to not have obtained the inheritance God has for us. In 2 Timothy 4:7–8, Paul says, "I have fought the good fight, I have finished the race, I have kept the faith. Now there is in store for me the crown of righteousness, which the Lord, the righteous Judge, will reward to me on that day—and not only to me, but also to all who have longed for his appearing." Are we fighting the good fight? Are we persevering in the faith? Are we looking toward the cross and awaiting the return of Christ? Are we living with that mind-set? Life can be hard—a reality that we all know. There are times when it feels like it's not going to get better, times when it doesn't feel like God is there or that He could possibly use what we're going through.

But don't give up! Don't lose sight of the goal! If your heart is breaking, so is God's. He may not rescue you from the situation, but you can trust that God is going through it with you. Although you may not see it now, He has a purpose. Believing and not feeling, not seeing—*that*, my sister, is keeping the faith. When all the world around you is reveling in the allures of the enemy, and you are standing firm, *that* is keeping the faith. You are holding on to the certainty that all God has for you far surpasses the temporary satisfaction of the world. Keeping the faith. And in those moments, you're also fighting the good fight for the faith. I want to finish the race stronger than what I started. Don't you? Philippians 3:14 says, "I press on toward the goal to win the prize for which God has called me heavenward in Christ Jesus."

What is the common theme in both Philippians 3:14 and 2 Timothy 4:8?

Both passages speak to the heavenly reward that is waiting—the crown of righteousness (by the blood of Jesus) and the prize Himself, Jesus Christ. Doesn't that make you want to jump from the rooftops, declaring to the world what a wonderful Savior we have? Living the life of faith is not without reward; the true reward is waiting. In our instantaneous culture, we want what we want—and we want it now. We don't like to wait to receive what is coming for us. *But God.* In His perfect wisdom, Jesus journeys through life with us, enables us to keep our eyes on Him, and calls us heavenward to claim our prize.

Write Galatians 6:9.

Are you encouraged to hold tightly onto Jesus? He urges us to stay strong, to not give up because we will reap the harvest. It is in the journey that we learn and grow. What do you want your legacy to be, sister? We have but one life to live. How are you living it? For what do you want to be remembered? It is *never* too late to start fresh with Jesus. God can use any life that is surrendered to Him, regardless of how old you are or what your rap sheet of sin is. Don't let Satan convince you otherwise. Remember Joshua? He began fighting and clearing out the Promised Land when he was "very old." God truly sees the condition of your heart and your motives toward Him. Hebrews 11 is well known as being the Hall of Faith in scripture. Remember that Rahab is listed there. What will your legacy be?

If people were to remember you, what do you think they would say about you?

When all is said and done, what do you want people to say about you and your faith?

Every day, pray that God will make you into that person you just described. He searches the earth, looking for the ones whose hearts are fully surrendered to Him. There needn't be anything special about us for Him to use us. No, He wants our willing hearts. Then, as we live in obedience, we can watch what He is able to do with our lives. And we can be amazed by Him!

Pour out your heart to God, telling Him all you want to be for Him and asking for

His strength. Then close your prayer with a commitment to standing firm until the very end.

Oh, beloved Jesus,

How we thank you today for being who You are and allowing us to grow closer to You. Thank You for revealing Yourself to us. Thank You for showing us and changing us into who You want us to be. Lord, I pray that we don't give up. I pray that we stay strong to the end and keep our eyes on the prize to which You have called us. Help us to know in our hearts the truth that nothing in this life satisfies, apart from You. Help us to stand firm and to keep the faith. Help us to run this race of life fully surrendered to You—*because You are worth it!* Oh, how I love You. Fill our hearts to the fullest measure of You. Praise You, Lord.

In Your wonderful name I pray, amen.

WEEK SEVEN

Week seven is our reflective week. So many times we complete Bible studies and feel that we learned so much, but then we don't remember to reflect and apply what we have learned. In an effort to absorb what we have learned, week seven will be centered around a theme that we have studied in the last six weeks. It will be a time of prayer and fasting. I am excited to see how God will move and work this week as we focus our hearts to tune in to His voice.

Day 1

Theme: Recognizing our excuses that prevent us from being obedient to God, acknowledging our fears to step out in faith, and choosing to accept grace over guilt

At the beginning of the study, we asked this question: what made Joshua believe God? We studied the story of Rahab. We examined our hearts and evaluated ourselves on the faith thermometer of how we believe God. God is so faithful, even when we are faithless, even when He does wonderful things for us and we quickly forget.

Let's focus our hearts today in prayerfulness to not let our past failures and mistakes prevent God's work in our lives for the future, to have courage to stand strong and do what God has placed on our hearts to do, and to move forward in faith, believing God's promises to us and surrendering our will to His.

Use the next section to be honest before God, to be vulnerable, to confess, to commit, to surrender, to ask God for clarity and courage, and to say whatever God is laying on your heart, regarding failures, fears, and faith.

Dear God,

Amen.

Each day as we close, we will choose something significant and meaningful as it pertains to what we just prayed, from which to fast for the day. Choose to focus your heart in what God has said to you today during your time of fasting. Pick whatever you feel God is laying on your heart from which you should fast. It can be anything: breakfast, lunch, dinner, chocolate, coffee, soda, Facebook, texting, your cell phone, watching TV or movies—anything!

Write your fast for the day.

Day 2

Theme: Fearing God and focusing on His holiness and consecrating ourselves to Him

May we never lose sight of who God is and His holiness. May we never lose respect of the one, true, holy God. Be set apart for Him today. What needs to be removed from our lives in order for God to have forward movement in our lives?

Pour your heart out to Jesus, asking for His discernment and wisdom into areas of your life in which you need to remove or consecrate to Him. Acknowledge His holiness and the role it plays in your life. Praise Him for who He is, and thank Him for loving you so much that He made a way to have an intimate relationship with each one of us.

Dear God,

Amen.

Write your fast for the day here.

Day 3

Theme: Confession of sins

We don't always make this a priority in our prayer lives, do we? We may acknowledge it and make mention of "forgive me for where I messed up today," but how often, outside of when we really make a mess of things, do we focus our hearts toward God and ask Him to reveal to us areas of our sins? How often are we specific about what sins we are confessing? Today we are going to focus on the confessions of our sins. Confess areas of unforgiveness, hard-heartedness, a bad attitude, being judgmental, being rude or unkind, pride, greed, selfishness, disobedience, unbelief, or whatever it is that you feel God is prompting in your spirit. Ask Him to show you areas of which you're not aware. Trust God to be faithful to reveal it to you. Then praise Him for His forgiveness and goodness to you.

Dawn Keister

Dear God,

Amen.

Write your fast for the day here.

Day 4

Theme: Identifying idols, tearing down strongholds, and surrendering in battle

"For though we live in the world, we do not wage war as the world does. The weapons we fight with are not the weapons of the world. On the contrary, they have the divine power to demolish strongholds. We demolish arguments against every pretension that sets itself up against the knowledge of God, and we take captive every thought to make it obedient to Christ" (2 Corinthians 10:3–5).

Sister, we must remain on high alert to areas of our lives that are vulnerable to setting up idols. The enemy lurks about, well familiar with our personal weaknesses. Then he goes for it! He maneuvers and manipulates in such a way that it resembles truth on the surface. Today, take this time of prayer to reflect on what may be an idol, what has the potential for being an idol, and areas of strongholds, and then surrender them. Lay down the white flag to Jesus, and then let His Holy Spirit claim the victory and power over your life. As you choose your area of fasting today, consider making it something that represents your stronghold or battle.

Dear God,

Amen.

Write your fast for the day here.

Day 5

Theme: Claiming your inheritance and remaining faithful

It is all for Jesus. He is the Alpha and the Omega, the beginning and the end. He is sovereign over all the in between. Praise Him. All that we are and all that we do means nothing apart from Jesus. The purpose of life is not to live and then die. God's timing in our lives—in choosing to place us here at this exact moment, in placing you in this study right now—is not an accident. God wants us to live our lives in the fullness of Him, journeying through the good days and the bad days with Him. Psalm 139 reveals to us the intimacy He longs to have with us today. When we claim our full inheritance in heaven, the days we have spent with Him here will be all the more precious because we will see Him face to face.

When the days of life seem overwhelming and heartbreaking, and you feel like you just can't go on anymore, remain faithful to Jesus because He is faithful to you. Even in the darkest days, He will never leave your side. Claim your inheritance today. As you pray today, I encourage to personalize Psalm 139 as a prayer to God. Thank God for being the Promised Land. Ask God for the strength and endurance to remain faithful to the end, until the day when your faith is made sight.

Dear God,

Amen.

Write your fast for the day here.

As we finish this Bible study together, my heart is full of gratitude, humility, and sadness that it's coming to a close. Thank you for joining me on this journey. Without Jesus, none of it is possible. I encourage you to walk in the abundance of your Promised Land as you continue your journey with Jesus. Never forget what He has taught you. Remember, He is absolutely worth it!

ENDNOTES

1   Spiros Zodhiates, ThD, ed., *Hebrew-Greek Key Word Study Bibles* (Chattanooga, TN: AMG Publishers, 1996), 1547.

2   Ibid., 1521.

3   Ibid., 1525.

4   Ibid, 1558.

5   Ibid., 1660.

6   John MacArthur, *The MacArthur Bible Commentary* (Nashville, TN: Thomas Nelson, Inc., 2005), 263.

7   Ibid., 264.

8   *Merriam-Webster*, s.v. "idol," accessed April 15, 2017, https://www.merriam-webster.com/dictionary/idol.

9   Zodhiates, *Key Word Study Bibles*, 1648.

Printed in the United States
By Bookmasters